NATIONAL CENTER FOR EDUCATION STATISTICS

ADULT LITERACY
in America

A First Look at the Results of the
National Adult Literacy Survey

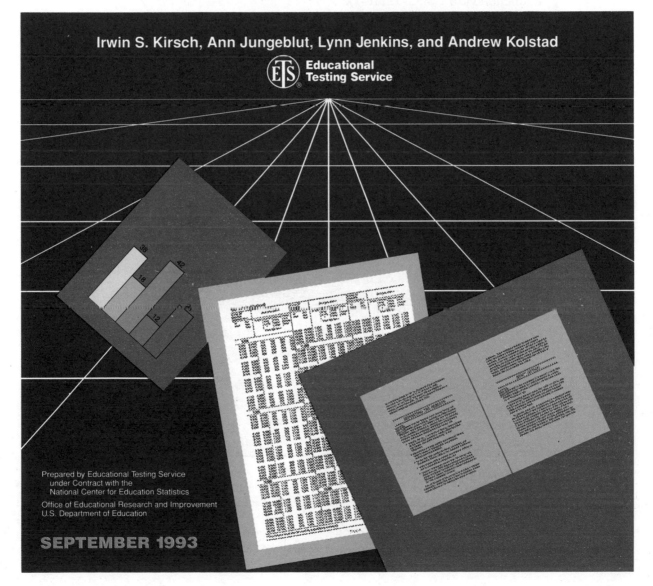

Irwin S. Kirsch, Ann Jungeblut, Lynn Jenkins, and Andrew Kolstad

ETS Educational Testing Service

Prepared by Educational Testing Service
under Contract with the
National Center for Education Statistics

Office of Educational Research and Improvement
U.S. Department of Education

SEPTEMBER 1993

U.S. Department of Education

Richard W. Riley
Secretary

Office of Educational Research and Improvement

Sharon P. Robinson
Assistant Secretary

National Center for Education Statistics

Emerson J. Elliott
Commissioner

National Center for Education Statistics

"The purpose of the Center shall be to collect, analyze, and disseminate statistics and other data related to education in the United States and in other nations." — Section 406(b) of the General Education Provisions Act, as amended (20 U.S.C. 1221e-1).

SEPTEMBER 1993

Contact: Andrew Kolstad, 202-219-1773

Ordering Information

For information on the price of single copies or bulk quantities of this book, call the U.S. Government Printing Office Order Desk at 202-783-3238.

The GPO stock number for this book is 065-000-00588-3

For more information,

write to:
Education Information Branch
Office of Educational Research and Improvement
U.S. Department of Education
555 New Jersey Avenue, N.W.
Washington, D.C. 20208-5641

or call:
1-800-424-1616
(in the Washington, D.C. metropolitan area, call 202-219-1651), or FAX 202-219-1970.

ISBN 0-16-041929-8

The work upon which this publication is based was performed for the National Center for Education Statistics, Office of Educational Research and Improvement, by Educational Testing Service.

Educational Testing Service is an equal opportunity, affirmative action employer.

Educational Testing Service, *ETS*, and ⓔⓣⓢ are registered trademarks of Educational Testing Service.

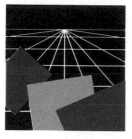

CONTENTS

Figures and Tables

ACKNOWLEDGMENTS

We extend our deep appreciation to the many individuals who contributed to this project and helped to create this first report on the results. In particular, thanks are due to the members of the Literacy Definition Committee, the Technical Review Committee, the Literacy of Older Adults Review Group, and the Literacy of Incarcerated Adults Review Group. These individuals, whose names appear in the appendices, guided the project from beginning to end, and we enjoyed the opportunity to collaborate with them.

NALS was a cooperative effort planned by the National Center for Education Statistics and the Division of Adult Education and Literacy, of the U.S. Department of Education. Emerson Elliott, commissioner, provided consistent support and guidance. We also thank Gary Phillips, Sue Ahmed, Joan Seamon, and Ron Pugsley, who played crucial roles in the project.

Thanks to our colleagues at Westat, Inc., for their outstanding work in managing the complex sampling, data collection, and composite weighting processes for the survey. We especially wish to thank project director Martha Berlin, senior statistician Joe Waksberg, statisticians Leyla Mohadjer and Jim Green, field director Sue Rieger, and field managers Rich Hilpert, Merle Klein, Judy Meader, and Cindy Randall. The hundreds of field supervisors and interviewers who carried out the survey deserve special thanks for their efforts. We are grateful to Renee Slobasky, senior vice president of Westat, for her continuing support.

At Educational Testing Service, we wish to thank Sam Messick for serving as corporate officer for the survey. Anne Campbell deserves special recognition for her excellent work in leading test development activities and managing the scoring and processing of the assessment materials. Mary Michaels coordinated the committee meetings, the publication of the assessment framework booklet, and other aspects of the project, ensuring that the work proceeded smoothly.

Doug Rhodes coordinated the state adult literacy survey project as well as printing and shipping operations for the national survey, assisted by Cathy Shaughnessy. Jules Goodison provided senior guidance and support, particularly in the operations process, and we are grateful to him for his many contributions. We would also like to express our appreciation to Dave Hobson for his sense in financial and other matters.

Our thanks go to all those who carried out the enormous volume of operations work — in particular, Debbie Giannacio, who ably coordinated the receipt of the survey materials, followup activities, and quality control. She was assisted by Kathy Miller, who also provided administrative support for the project. We acknowledge the contributions of Joanne Antonoff, who helped prepare the NALS proposal and whose memory we cherish.

We thank Don Rock and Kentaro Yamamoto of Educational Testing Service, who directed the statistical and psychometric activities and provided invaluable guidance on technical matters. Robert Mislevy helped us reflect on statistical as well as philosophical questions, and we are grateful for his contributions. Charlie Lewis, Neal Thomas, and Min hwei Wang were available for statistical advice.

Norma Norris deserves special honors for conducting the statistical work and managing the data analyses under impossibly tight deadlines. Her support went above and beyond the call of duty, and we are grateful for her dedication to the project. Additional thanks are extended to Jim Ferris, Dave Freund, Tom Jirele, Bruce Kaplan, Jennifer Nelson, Inge Novatkoski, Kate Pashley, and Lois Worthington, who shared responsibility for conducting the data analyses. Thanks to John Barone for helping to oversee data analysis activities.

As this report took shape, many reviewers asked questions and provided insights that helped us sharpen our thinking and writing. In particular, we wish to thank Kent Ashworth, Paul Barton, Anne Campbell, Archie Lapointe, Peter Mosenthal, and Ron Solarzano for their suggestions. We also appreciate the thoughtful comments we received from the government's reviewers, including Nabeel Alsalam, Janet Baldwin, John Burkett, Ruth Childs, Mary Anne Nester, Linda Roberts, Peter Stowe, and David Sweet.

Beverly Cisney provided invaluable assistance in word processing and desktop publishing for this report. Her commitment to the project is appreciated.

We also extend many thanks to Susan Busfield, who designed and prepared the tables and graphs for this report under the most difficult deadlines. Thanks also go to the test development consultants, whose names are listed at the end of the report, and to the individuals who scored the responses to the assessment tasks.

Producing this report was a challenge, and it would not have been possible without the excellent work of the ETS Publications Division. In particular, we thank Robin Matlack, who conceived the beautiful design for the report; Joyce Martorelli, who typeset the manuscript; Peter Stremic, who ensured that the report met the highest standards; Fred Marx, who managed the production stages; Kathy Benischeck, who coordinated the production process; and Kiyo Toma, who answered our technical questions. We thank editors Shilpi Niyogi and Carol Carlson for their careful reviews of the manuscript.

Finally, we wish to thank the thousands of adults across the country who gave their time to respond to the survey. Without their participation, this study would not have been possible.

Irwin S. Kirsch	Lynn Jenkins
Ann Jungeblut	Andrew Kolstad

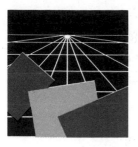

PREFACE

The United States has always been a mosaic of cultures, but the diversity of our population has increased by striking proportions in recent years. As Barbara Everitt Bryant, director of the Bureau of the Census, has written: "If you gave America a face in 1990, it would have shown the first sign of wrinkles [and] it would have been full of color."[1] The median age of Americans continues to rise, growing from 30 to almost 33 years during the 1980s. It is projected that by the year 2080, nearly 25 percent of the adults in this nation will be over 65, compared with only about 12 percent today. The racial and ethnic composition of the nation also continues to change. While 3.7 million people of Asian or Pacific Islander origin were living in this country in 1980, there were 7.2 million a decade later — a change of almost 100 percent. The number of individuals of Hispanic origin also rose dramatically over this time period, from roughly 6 to 9 percent of the population, or more than 22 million people. Our increasing diversity can not only be seen but also heard: today, some 32 million individuals in the United States speak a language other than English, and these languages range from Spanish and Chinese to Yupik and Mon-Khmer.[2]

Given these patterns and changes, this is an opportune time to explore the literacy skills of adults in this nation. In 1988, the U.S. Congress called on the Department of Education to support a national literacy survey of America's adults. While recent studies funded by the federal government explored the literacy of young adults and job seekers, the National Adult Literacy Survey is the first to provide accurate and detailed information on the skills of the adult population as a whole — information that, to this point, has been unavailable.

Perhaps never before have so many people from so many different sectors of society been concerned about adult literacy. Numerous reports published in

---

[1] B.E. Bryant. (1991). "The Changing Face of the United States." *The World Almanac and Book of Facts, 1992.* New York, NY: Pharos Books. p. 72.

[2] United States Department of Commerce. (1993, April). "Number of Non-English Language Speaking Americans Up Sharply in 1980s, Census Bureau Says." *United States Department of Commerce News.*

the last decade — including *A Nation at Risk*, *The Bottom Line*, *The Subtle Danger*, *Literacy: Profiles of America's Young Adults*, *Jump Start: The Federal Role in Adult Education*, *Workforce 2000*, *America's Choice: High Skills or Low Wages*, and *Beyond the School Doors* — have provided evidence that a large portion of our population lacks adequate literacy skills and have intensified the debate over how this problem should be addressed.

Concerns about literacy are not new. In fact, throughout our nation's history there have been periods when the literacy skills of the population were judged inadequate. Yet, the nature of these concerns has changed radically over time. In the past, the lack of ability to read and use printed materials was seen primarily as an individual problem, with implications for a person's job opportunities, educational goals, sense of fulfillment, and participation in society. Now, however, it is increasingly viewed as a national problem, with implications that reach far beyond the individual. Concerns about the human costs of limited literacy have, in a sense, been overshadowed by concerns about the economic and social costs.

Although Americans today are, on the whole, better educated and more literate than any who preceded them, many employers say they are unable to find enough workers with the reading, writing, mathematical, and other competencies required in the workplace. Changing economic, demographic, and labor-market forces may exacerbate the problem in the future. As a recent study by the American Society for Training and Development concluded, "These forces are creating a human capital deficit that threatens U.S. competitiveness and acts as a barrier to individual opportunities for all Americans."[3]

Whether future jobs will have greater literacy requirements than today's jobs, or whether the gap between the nation's literacy resources and its needs will widen, are open questions. The evidence to support such predictions is scarce. What many believe, however, is that our current systems of education and training are inadequate to ensure individual opportunities, improve economic productivity, or strengthen our nation's competitiveness in the global marketplace.

There is widespread agreement that we as a nation must respond to the literacy challenge, not only to preserve our economic vitality but also to ensure that every individual has a full range of opportunities for personal fulfillment and participation in society. At the historic education summit in Charlottesville, Virginia, the nation's governors — including then-Governor Clinton — met with then-President Bush to establish a set of national education goals that would guide this country into the twenty-first century. As adopted in 1990 by members of the National Governors' Association, one of the six goals states:

---

[3] A.P. Carnevale, L.J. Gainer, A.S. Meltzer, and S.L. Holland. (1988, October). "Workplace Basics: The Skills Employers Want." *Training and Development Journal.* pp. 20-30.

By the year 2000, every adult American will be
literate and will possess the knowledge and skills
necessary to compete in a global economy and
exercise the rights and responsibilities of citizenship.

The following year, Congress passed the National Literacy Act of 1991, the purpose of which is "to enhance the literacy and basic skills of adults, to ensure that all adults in the United States acquire the basic skills necessary to function effectively and achieve the greatest possible opportunity in their work and in their lives, and to strengthen and coordinate adult literacy programs."

But how should these ambitious goals be pursued? In the past, whenever the population's skills were called into question, critics generally focused on the educational system and insisted that school reforms were necessary if the nation were to escape serious social and economic consequences. Today, however, many of those who need to improve their literacy skills have already left school. In fact, it is estimated that almost 80 percent of the work force for the year 2000 is already employed. Moreover, many of those who demonstrate limited literacy skills do not perceive that they have a problem. Clearly, then, the schools alone cannot strengthen the abilities of present and future employees, and of the population as a whole. A broad-based response seems necessary.

To initiate such a response, we need more than localized reports or anecdotal information from employers, public leaders, or the press; accurate and detailed information about our current status is essential. As reading researchers John Carroll and Jean Chall observed in their book *Toward a Literate Society*, "any national program for improving literacy skills would have to be based on the best possible information as to where the deficits are and how serious they are."[4] Surprisingly, though, we do lack accurate and detailed information about literacy in our nation — including how many individuals have limited skills, who they are, and the severity of their problems.

In 1988, Congress asked the U.S. Department of Education to address this need for information on the nature and extent of adult literacy. In response, the Department's National Center for Education Statistics and Division of Adult Education and Literacy called for a national household survey of the literacy skills of adults in the United States. A contract was awarded to Educational Testing Service and a subcontract to Westat, Inc. to design and conduct the National Adult Literacy Survey, the results of which are presented in these pages.

---

[4] J.B. Carroll and J.S. Chall, eds. (1975). *Toward a Literate Society: A Report from the National Academy of Education*. New York, NY: McGraw-Hill. p. 11.

During the first eight months of 1992, trained staff conducted household interviews with nearly 13,600 individuals aged 16 and older who had been randomly selected to represent the adult population in this country. In addition, approximately 1,000 adults were surveyed in each of 12 states that chose to participate in a special study designed to produce state-level results that are comparable to the national data. Finally, some 1,100 inmates from 80 federal and state prisons were interviewed to gather information on the skills of the prison population. Each individual was asked to spend about an hour responding to a series of diverse literacy tasks and providing information on his or her background, education, labor market experiences, and reading practices.

The results of the National Adult Literacy Survey comprise an enormous set of data that includes more than a million responses to the literacy tasks and background questions. More important than the size of the database, however, is the fact that it provides information that was previously unavailable — information that is essential to understanding this nation's literacy resources.

To ensure that the survey results will reach a wide audience, the committees that guided the project recommended that the findings be issued in a series of reports. This first volume in the series offers an overview of the results. Additional reports offer a more detailed look at particular issues that are explored in a general way in this report, including:

● literacy in the work force

● literacy and education

● literacy among older adults

● literacy in the prison population

● literacy and cultural diversity

● literacy practices

A final report conveys technical information about the survey design and the methods used to implement it.

Although these reports focus almost exclusively on the results of the National Adult Literacy Survey, their contents have much broader implications. The rich collection of information they contain can be used to inform policy debates, set program objectives, and reflect on our society's literacy resources and needs.

Irwin S. Kirsch
Project Director

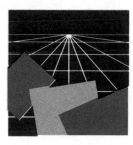

EXECUTIVE SUMMARY

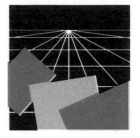

EXECUTIVE SUMMARY

This report provides a first look at the results of the National Adult Literacy Survey, a project funded by the U.S. Department of Education and administered by Educational Testing Service, in collaboration with Westat, Inc. It provides the most detailed portrait that has ever been available on the condition of literacy in this nation — and on the unrealized potential of its citizens.

Many past studies of adult literacy have tried to count the number of "illiterates" in this nation, thereby treating literacy as a condition that individuals either do or do not have. We believe that such efforts are inherently arbitrary and misleading. They are also damaging, in that they fail to acknowledge both the complexity of the literacy problem and the range of solutions needed to address it.

The National Adult Literacy Survey (NALS) is based on a different definition of literacy, and therefore follows a different approach to measuring it. The aim of this survey is to profile the English literacy of adults in the United States based on their performance across a wide array of tasks that reflect the types of materials and demands they encounter in their daily lives.

To gather the information on adults' literacy skills, trained staff interviewed nearly 13,600 individuals aged 16 and older during the first eight months of 1992. These participants had been randomly selected to represent the adult population in the country as a whole. In addition, about 1,000 adults were surveyed in each of 12 states that chose to participate in a special study designed to provide state-level results that are comparable to the national data. Finally, some 1,100 inmates from 80 federal and state prisons were interviewed to gather information on the proficiencies of the prison population. In total, over 26,000 adults were surveyed.

Each survey participant was asked to spend approximately an hour responding to a series of diverse literacy tasks as well as questions about his or her demographic characteristics, educational background, reading practices, and other areas related to literacy. Based on their responses to the survey tasks, adults received proficiency scores along three scales which reflect varying degrees of skill in prose, document, and quantitative literacy. The scales are powerful tools which make it possible to explore the proportions of adults in various subpopulations of interest who demonstrated successive levels of performance.

This report describes the types and levels of literacy skills demonstrated by adults in this country and analyzes the variation in skills across major subgroups in the population. It also explores connections between literacy skills and social and economic variables such as voting, economic status, weeks worked, and earnings. Some of the major findings are highlighted here.

The Literacy Skills of America's Adults

- Twenty-one to 23 percent — or some 40 to 44 million of the 191 million adults in this country — demonstrated skills in the lowest level of prose, document, and quantitative proficiencies (Level 1). Though all adults in this level displayed limited skills, their characteristics are diverse. Many adults in this level performed simple, routine tasks involving brief and uncomplicated texts and documents. For example, they were able to total an entry on a deposit slip, locate the time or place of a meeting on a form, and identify a piece of specific information in a brief news article. Others were unable to perform these types of tasks, and some had such limited skills that they were unable to respond to much of the survey.

- Many factors help to explain why so many adults demonstrated English literacy skills in the lowest proficiency level defined (Level 1). Twenty-five percent of the respondents who performed in this level were immigrants who may have been just learning to speak English. Nearly two-thirds of those in Level 1 (62 percent) had terminated their education before completing high school. A third were age 65 or older, and 26 percent had physical, mental, or health conditions that kept them from participating fully in work, school, housework, or other activities. Nineteen percent of the respondents in Level 1 reported having visual difficulties that affect their ability to read print.

- Some 25 to 28 percent of the respondents, representing about 50 million adults nationwide, demonstrated skills in the next higher level of proficiency (Level 2) on each of the literacy scales. While their skills were more varied than those of individuals performing in Level 1, their repertoire was still quite limited. They were generally able to locate information in text, to make low-level inferences using printed materials, and to integrate easily identifiable pieces of information. Further, they demonstrated the ability to perform quantitative tasks that involve a single operation where the numbers are either stated or can be easily found in text. For example, adults in this level were able to calculate the total cost of a purchase or determine the difference in price between two items. They could also locate a particular intersection on a street map and enter background information on a simple form.

- Individuals in Levels 1 and 2 were much less likely to respond correctly to the more challenging literacy tasks in the assessment — those requiring higher level reading and problem-solving skills. In particular, they were apt to experience considerable difficulty in performing tasks that required them to integrate or synthesize information from complex or lengthy texts or to perform quantitative tasks that involved two or more sequential operations and in which the individual had to set up the problem.

- The approximately 90 million adults who performed in Levels 1 and 2 did not necessarily perceive themselves as being "at risk." Across the literacy scales, 66 to 75 percent of the adults in the lowest level and 93 to 97 percent in the second lowest level described themselves as being able to read or write English "well" or "very well." Moreover, only 14 to 25 percent of the adults in Level 1 and 4 to 12 percent in Level 2 said they get a lot of help from family members or friends with everyday prose, document, and quantitative literacy tasks. It is therefore possible that their skills, while limited, allow them to meet some or most of their personal and occupational literacy needs.

- Nearly one-third of the survey participants, or about 61 million adults nationwide, demonstrated performance in Level 3 on each of the literacy scales. Respondents performing in this level on the prose and document scales were able to integrate information from relatively long or dense text or from documents. Those in the third level on the quantitative scale were able to determine the appropriate arithmetic operation based on information contained in the directive, and to identify the quantities needed to perform that operation.

- Eighteen to 21 percent of the respondents, or 34 to 40 million adults, performed in the two highest levels of prose, document, and quantitative literacy (Levels 4 and 5). These adults demonstrated proficiencies associated with the most challenging tasks in this assessment, many of which involved long and complex documents and text passages.

- The literacy proficiencies of young adults assessed in 1992 were somewhat lower, on average, than the proficiencies of young adults who participated in a 1985 literacy survey. NALS participants aged 21 to 25 had average prose, document, and quantitative scores that were 11 to 14 points lower than the scores of 21- to 25-year-olds assessed in 1985. Although other factors may also be involved, these performance discrepancies are probably due in large part to changes in the demographic composition of the population — in particular, the dramatic increase in the percentages of young Hispanic adults, many of whom were born in other countries and are learning English as a second language.

- Adults with relatively few years of education were more likely to perform in the lower literacy levels than those who completed high school or received some type of postsecondary education. For example, on each of the three literacy scales, some 75 to 80 percent of adults with 0 to 8 years of education are in Level 1, while fewer than 1 percent are in Levels 4 and 5. In contrast, among adults with a high school diploma, 16 to 20 percent are in the lowest level on each scale, while 10 to 13 percent are in the two highest levels. Only 4 percent of adults with four year college degrees are in Level 1; 44 to 50 percent are in the two highest levels.

- Older adults were more likely than middle-aged and younger adults to demonstrate limited literacy skills. For example, adults over the age of 65 have average literacy scores that range from 56 to 61 points (or more than one level) below those of adults 40 to 54 years of age. Adults aged 55 to 64 scored, on average, between middle-aged adults and those 65 years and older. These differences can be explained in part by the fact that older adults tend to have completed fewer years of schooling than adults in the younger age groups.

- Black, American Indian/Alaskan Native, Hispanic, and Asian/Pacific Islander adults were more likely than White adults to perform in the lowest two literacy levels. These performance differences are affected by many factors. For example, with the exception of Asian/Pacific Islander adults, individuals in these groups tended to have completed fewer years of schooling in this country than had White individuals. Further, many adults of Asian/Pacific Islander and Hispanic origin were born in other countries and were likely to have learned English as a second language.

- Of all the racial/ethnic groups, Hispanic adults reported the fewest years of schooling in this country (just over 10 years, on average). The average years of schooling attained by Black adults and American Indian/Alaskan Native adults were similar, at 11.6 and 11.7 years, respectively. These groups had completed more years of schooling than Hispanic adults had, on average, but more than a year less than either White adults or those of Asian/Pacific Islander origin.

- With one exception, for each racial or ethnic group, individuals born in the United States outperformed those born abroad. The exception occurs among Black adults, where there was essentially no difference (only 3 to 7 points). Among White and Asian/Pacific Islander adults, the average differences between native-born and foreign-born individuals range from 26 to 41 points across the literacy scales. Among Hispanic adults, the differences range from 40 to 94 points in favor of the native born.

- Twelve percent of the respondents reported having a physical, mental, or other health condition that kept them from participating fully in work or other activities. These individuals were far more likely than adults in the population as a whole to demonstrate performance in the range for Levels 1 and 2. Among those who said they had vision problems, 54 percent were in Level 1 on the prose scale and another 26 percent were in Level 2.

- Men demonstrated the same average prose proficiencies as women, but their document and quantitative proficiencies were somewhat higher. Adults in the Midwest and West had higher average proficiencies than those residing in either the Northeast or South.

- Adults in prison were far more likely than those in the population as a whole to perform in the lowest two literacy levels. These incarcerated adults tended to be younger, less well educated, and to be from minority backgrounds.

Literacy and Social and Economic Characteristics

- Individuals demonstrating higher levels of literacy were more likely to be employed, work more weeks in a year, and earn higher wages than individuals demonstrating lower proficiencies. For example, while adults in Level 1 on each scale reported working an average of only 18 to 19 weeks in the year prior to the survey, those in the three highest levels reported working about twice as many weeks — between 34 and 44. Moreover, across the scales, individuals in the lowest level reported median weekly earnings of about $230 to $245, compared with about $350 for individuals performing in Level 3 and $620 to $680 for those in Level 5.

- Adults in the lowest level on each of the literacy scales (17 to 19 percent) were far more likely than those in the two highest levels (4 percent) to report receiving food stamps. In contrast, only 23 to 27 percent of the respondents who performed in Level 1 said they received interest from a savings or bank account, compared with 70 to 85 percent in Levels 4 or 5.

- Nearly half (41 to 44 percent) of all adults in the lowest level on each literacy scale were living in poverty, compared with only 4 to 8 percent of those in the two highest proficiency levels.

- On all three literacy scales, adults in the higher levels were more likely than those in the lower levels to report voting in a recent state or national election. Slightly more than half (55 to 58 percent) of the adults in Level 1 who were eligible to vote said they voted in the past five years, compared with about 80 percent of those who performed in Level 4 and nearly 90 percent of those in Level 5.

Reflections on the Results

In reflecting on the results of the National Adult Literacy Survey, many readers will undoubtedly seek an answer to a fundamental question: Are the literacy skills of America's adults adequate? That is, are the distributions of prose, document, and quantitative proficiency observed in this survey adequate to ensure individual opportunities for all adults, to increase worker productivity, or to strengthen America's competitiveness around the world?

Because it is impossible to say precisely what literacy skills are essential for individuals to succeed in this or any other society, the results of the National Adult Literacy Survey provide no firm answers to such questions. As the authors examined the survey data and deliberated on the results with members of the advisory committees, however, several observations and concerns emerged.

Perhaps the most salient finding of this survey is that such large percentages of adults performed in the lowest levels (Levels 1 and 2) of prose, document, and quantitative literacy. In and of itself, this may not indicate a serious problem. After all, the majority of adults who demonstrated limited skills described themselves as reading or writing English well, and relatively few said they get a lot of assistance from others in performing everyday literacy tasks. Perhaps these individuals are able to meet most of the literacy demands they encounter currently at work, at home, and in their communities.

Yet, some argue that lower literacy skills mean a lower quality of life and more limited employment opportunities. As noted in a recent report from the American Society for Training and Development, "The association between skills and opportunity for individual Americans is powerful and growing. . . . Individuals with poor skills do not have much to bargain with; they are condemned to low earnings and limited choices."[i]

The data from this survey appear to support such views. On each of the literacy scales, adults whose proficiencies were within the two lowest levels were far less likely than their more literate peers to be employed full-time, to earn high wages, and to vote. Moreover, they were far more likely to receive food stamps, to be in poverty, and to rely on nonprint sources (such as radio and television) for information about current events, public affairs, and government.

Literacy is not the only factor that contributes to how we live our lives, however. Some adults who displayed limited skills reported working in professional or managerial jobs, earning high wages, and participating in various aspects of our society, for example, while others who demonstrated high levels of proficiency reported being unemployed or out of the labor force. Thus, having advanced literacy skills does not necessarily guarantee individual opportunities.

Still, literacy can be thought of as a currency in this society. Just as adults with little money have difficulty meeting their basic needs, those with limited literacy skills are likely to find it more challenging to pursue their goals — whether these involve job advancement, consumer decisionmaking, citizenship, or other aspects of their lives. Even if adults who performed in the lowest literacy levels are not experiencing difficulties at present, they may be at risk as the nation's economy and social fabric continue to change.

Beyond these personal consequences, what implications are there for society when so many individuals display limited skills? The answer to this question is elusive. Still, it seems apparent that a nation in which large numbers of citizens display limited literacy skills has fewer resources with which to meet its goals and objectives, whether these are social, political, civic, or economic.

If large percentages of adults had to do little more than be able to sign their name on a form or locate a single fact in a newspaper or table, then the levels of literacy seen in this survey might not warrant concern. We live in a nation, however, where both the volume and variety of written information are growing and where increasing numbers of citizens are expected to be able to read, understand, and use these materials.

---

[i] A.J. Carnevale and L.J. Gainer. (1989). *The Learning Enterprise*. Washington, DC: U.S. Department of Labor, Employment and Training Administration.

Historians remind us that during the last 200 hundred years, our nation's literacy skills have increased dramatically in response to new requirements and expanded opportunities for social and economic growth. Today we are a better educated and more literate society than at any time in our history.[2] Yet, there have also been periods of imbalance — times when demands seemed to surpass levels of attainment.

In recent years, our society has grown more technologically advanced and the roles of formal institutions have expanded. As this has occurred, many have argued that there is a greater need for all individuals to become more literate and for a larger proportion to develop advanced skills.[3] Growing numbers of individuals are expected to be able to attend to multiple features of information in lengthy and sometimes complex displays, to compare and contrast information, to integrate information from various parts of a text or document, to generate ideas and information based on what they read, and to apply arithmetic operations sequentially to solve a problem.

The results from this and other surveys, however, indicate that many adults do not demonstrate these levels of proficiency. Further, the continuing process of demographic, social, and economic change within this country could lead to a more divided society along both racial and socioeconomic lines.

Already there is evidence of a widening division. According to the report *America's Choice: High Skills or Low Wages!*, over the past 15 years the gap in earnings between professionals and clerical workers has grown from 47 to 86 percent while the gap between white collar workers and skilled tradespeople has risen from 2 to 37 percent. At the same time, earnings for college educated males 24 to 34 years of age have increased by 10 percent while earnings for those with high school diplomas have declined by 9 percent. Moreover, the poverty rate for Black families is nearly three times that for White families.[4] One child in five is born into poverty, and for minority populations, this rate approaches one in two.

---

[2] L.C. Stedman and C.F. Kaestle. (1991). "Literacy and Reading Performance in the United States from 1880 to the Present," in C.F. Kaestle et al., *Literacy in the United States: Readers and Reading Since 1880*. New Haven, CT: Yale University Press. T. Snyder (ed.). (1993). *120 Years of American Education: A Statistical Portrait*. Washington, DC: National Center for Education Statistics.

[3] U.S. Department of Labor. (1992, April). *Learning a Living: A Blueprint for High Performance*. Washington, DC: The Secretary's Commission on Achieving Necessary Skills (SCANS). R.L. Venezky, C.F. Kaestle, and A. Sum. (1987, January). *The Subtle Danger: Reflections on the Literacy Abilities of America's Young Adults*. Princeton, NJ: Educational Testing Service.

[4] National Center on Education and the Economy. (1990, June). *America's Choice: High Skills or Low Wages! The Report of The Commission on the Skills of the American Workforce.* p. 20.

In 1990, then-President Bush and the nation's governors, including then-Governor Clinton, adopted the goal that *all* of America's adults be literate by the year 2000. The responsibility for meeting this objective must, in the end, be shared among individuals, groups, and organizations throughout our society. Programs that serve adult learners cannot be expected to solve the literacy problem alone, and neither can the schools. Other institutions — ranging from the largest and most complex government agency, to large and small businesses, to the family — all have a role to play in ensuring that adults who need or wish to improve their literacy skills have the opportunity to do so. It is also important that individuals themselves come to realize the value of literacy in their lives and to recognize the benefits associated with having better skills. Only then will more adults in this nation develop the literacy resources they need to function in society, to achieve their goals, and to develop their knowledge and potential.

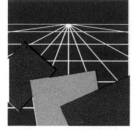

INTRODUCTION

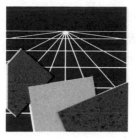

INTRODUCTION

Development is a process that increases choices. It creates an environment where people can exercise their full potential to lead productive, creative lives. . . . At the heart of development is literacy — the ability to recognize, interpret, and act on symbolic representations of our world through various forms of language and cultural expression. Facility in manipulating these symbols, whether through the written word, numbers or images, is essential to effective human development. Thus, meeting the basic learning needs of all is a major goal of sustainable and lasting improvement in the human condition.

— *William H. Drapper III, Letters of Life*

Few would deny the importance of literacy in this society or the advantages enjoyed by those with advanced skills. This shared belief in the value of literacy, though, does not imply consensus on the ways it should be defined and measured. In fact, opinions vary widely about the skills that individuals need to function successfully in their work, in their personal lives, and in society, and about the ways in which these skills should be assessed. As a result, there have been widely conflicting diagnoses of the literacy problem in this country. The National Adult Literacy Survey was initiated to fill the need for accurate and detailed information on the English literacy skills of America's adults.

In the Adult Education Amendments of 1988, the U.S. Congress called upon the Department of Education to report on the definition of literacy and on the nature and extent of literacy among adults in the nation. In response, the Department's National Center for Education Statistics (NCES) and the Division of Adult Education and Literacy planned a national household survey of adult literacy. In September 1989, NCES awarded a four-year contract to Educational Testing Service (ETS) to design and administer the survey and to analyze and report the results. A subcontract was given to Westat, Inc., for sampling and field operations.

The plan for developing and conducting the National Adult Literacy Survey (NALS) was guided by a panel of experts from business and industry, labor, government, research, and adult education. This Literacy Definition Committee worked with ETS staff to prepare a definition of literacy that would guide the development of the assessment objectives as well as the construction and selection of assessment tasks. A second panel, the Technical Review Committee, was formed to help ensure the soundness of the assessment design, the quality of the data collected, the integrity of the analyses conducted, and the appropriateness of the interpretations of the final results.

This introduction summarizes the discussions that led to the adoption of a definition of literacy for the National Adult Literacy Survey, the framework used in designing the survey instruments, the populations assessed, the survey administration, and the methods for reporting the results.

Defining and Measuring Literacy

The National Adult Literacy Survey is the third and largest assessment of adult literacy funded by the federal government and conducted by ETS. The two previous efforts included a 1985 household survey of the literacy skills of 21- to 25-year-olds, funded by the U.S. Department of Education, and a 1989-90 survey of the literacy proficiencies of job seekers, funded by the U.S. Department of Labor.[1] The definition of literacy that guided the National Adult Literacy Survey was rooted in these preceding studies.

Building on earlier work in large-scale literacy assessment, the 1985 young adult survey attempted to extend the concept of literacy, to take into account some of the criticisms of previous surveys, and to benefit from advances in educational assessment methodology. The national panel of experts that was assembled to construct a definition of literacy for this survey rejected the types of arbitrary standards — such as signing one's name, completing five years of school, or scoring at a particular grade level on a school-based measure of reading achievement — that have long been used to make judgements about adults' literacy skills. Through a consensus process, this panel drafted the following definition of literacy, which helped set the framework for the young adult survey:

> *Using printed and written information to function in society, to achieve one's goals, and to develop one's knowledge and potential.*

---

[1] I.S. Kirsch and A. Jungeblut. (1986). *Literacy: Profiles of America's Young Adults*. Princeton, NJ: Educational Testing Service. I.S. Kirsch, A. Jungeblut, and A. Campbell. (1992). *Beyond the School Doors: The Literacy Needs of Job Seekers Served by the U.S. Department of Labor*. Princeton, NJ: Educational Testing Service.

Unlike traditional definitions of literacy, which focused on decoding and comprehension, this definition encompasses a broad range of skills that adults use in accomplishing the many different types of literacy tasks associated with work, home, and community contexts. This perspective is shaping not only adult literacy assessment, but policy, as well — as seen in the National Literacy Act of 1991, which defined literacy as "an individual's ability to read, write, and speak in English and compute and solve problems at levels of proficiency necessary to function on the job and in society, to achieve one's goals, and to develop one's knowledge and potential."

The definition of literacy from the young adult survey was adopted by the panel that guided the development of the 1989-90 survey of job seekers, and it also provided the starting point for the discussions of the NALS Literacy Definition Committee. This committee agreed that expressing the literacy proficiencies of adults in school-based terms or grade-level scores is inappropriate. In addition, while the committee recognized the importance of teamwork skills, interpersonal skills, and communication skills for functioning in various contexts, such as the work place, it decided that these areas would not be addressed in this survey.

Further, the committee endorsed the notion that literacy is neither a single skill suited to all types of texts, nor an infinite number of skills, each associated with a given type of text or material. Rather, as suggested by the results of the young adult and job-seeker surveys, an ordered set of skills appears to be called into play to accomplish diverse types of tasks. Given this perspective, the NALS committee agreed to adopt not only the definition of literacy that was used in the previous surveys, but also the three scales developed as part of those efforts:

Prose literacy — the knowledge and skills needed to understand and use information from texts that include editorials, news stories, poems, and fiction; for example, finding a piece of information in a newspaper article, interpreting instructions from a warranty, inferring a theme from a poem, or contrasting views expressed in an editorial.

Document literacy — the knowledge and skills required to locate and use information contained in materials that include job applications, payroll forms, transportation schedules, maps, tables, and graphs; for example, locating a particular intersection on a street map, using a schedule to choose the appropriate bus, or entering information on an application form.

Quantitative literacy — the knowledge and skills required to apply arithmetic operations, either alone or sequentially, using numbers embedded in printed materials; for example, balancing a checkbook, figuring out a tip, completing an order form, or determining the amount of interest from a loan advertisement.

The literacy scales provide a useful way to organize a broad array of tasks and to report the assessment results. They represent a substantial improvement over traditional approaches to literacy assessment, which have tended to report on performance in terms of single tasks or to combine the results from diverse tasks into a single, conglomerate score. Such a score fosters the simplistic notion that "literates" and "illiterates" can be neatly distinguished from one another based on a single cutpoint on a single scale. The literacy scales, on the other hand, make it possible to profile the various types and levels of literacy among different subgroups in our society. In so doing, they help us to understand the diverse information-processing skills associated with the broad range of printed and written materials that adults read and their many purposes for reading them.

In adopting the three scales for use in this survey, the committee's aim was not to establish a single national standard for literacy. Rather, it was to provide an interpretive scheme that would enable levels of prose, document, and quantitative performance to be identified and allow descriptions of the knowledge and skills associated with each level to be developed.

The prose, document, and quantitative scales were built initially to report on the results of the young adult survey and were augmented in the survey of job seekers. The NALS Literacy Definition Committee recommended that a new set of literacy tasks be developed to enhance the scales. These tasks would take into account the following, without losing the ability to compare the NALS results to the earlier surveys:

- continued use of open-ended simulation tasks

- continued emphasis on tasks that measure a broad range of information-processing skills and cover a wide variety of contexts

- increased emphasis on simulation tasks that require brief written and/or oral responses

- increased emphasis on tasks that ask respondents to describe how they would set up and solve a problem

- the use of a simple, four-function calculator to solve selected quantitative problems

Approximately 110 new assessment tasks were field tested, and 80 of these were selected for inclusion in the survey, in addition to 85 tasks that were administered in both the young adult and job-seeker assessments. By administering a common set of simulation tasks in each of the three literacy surveys, it is possible to compare results across time and across population groups.

A large number of tasks had to be administered in NALS to ensure that the survey would provide the broadest possible coverage of the literacy domains specified. Yet, no individual could be expected to respond to the entire set of 165 simulation tasks. Accordingly, the survey was designed to give each person participating in the study a subset of the total pool of literacy tasks, while at the same time ensuring that each of the 165 tasks was administered to a nationally representative sample of adults. Literacy tasks were assigned to sections that could be completed in about 15 minutes, and these sections were then compiled into booklets, each of which could be completed in about 45 minutes. During a personal interview, each survey respondent was asked to complete one booklet.

In addition to the time allocated for the literacy tasks, approximately 20 minutes were devoted to obtaining background and personal information from respondents. Two versions of the background questionnaire were administered, one in English and one in Spanish. Major areas explored included: *background and demographics* — country of birth, languages spoken or read, access to reading materials, size of household, educational attainment of parents, age, race/ethnicity, and marital status; *education* — highest grade completed in school, current aspirations, participation in adult education classes, and education received outside the country; *labor market experiences* — employment status, recent labor market experiences, and occupation; *income* — personal as well as household; and *activities* — voting behavior, hours spent watching television, frequency and content of newspaper reading, and use of literacy skills for work and leisure. These background data make it possible to gain an understanding of the ways in which personal characteristics are associated with demonstrated performance on each of the three literacy scales.[2]

Conducting the Survey

NALS was conducted during the first eight months of 1992 with a nationally representative sample of some 13,600 adults. More than 400 trained interviewers, some of whom were bilingual in English and Spanish, visited nearly 27,000 households to select and interview adults aged 16 and older, each of whom was asked to provide personal and background information and to complete a booklet of literacy tasks. Black and Hispanic households were

---

[2] A more detailed description of the NALS design and framework can be found in an interim report: A. Campbell, I.S. Kirsch, and A. Kolstad. (1992, October). *Assessing Literacy: The Framework for the National Adult Literacy Survey*. Washington, DC: National Center for Education Statistics.

oversampled to ensure reliable estimates of literacy proficiencies and to permit analyses of the performance of these subpopulations.

To give states an opportunity to explore the skill levels of their populations, each of the 50 states was invited to participate in a concurrent assessment. While many states expressed an interest, 11 elected to participate in the State Adult Literacy Survey. Approximately 1,000 adults aged 16 to 64 were surveyed in each of the following states:

California	Louisiana	Pennsylvania
Illinois	New Jersey	Texas
Indiana	New York	Washington
Iowa	Ohio	

To permit comparisons of the state and national results, the survey instruments administered to the state and national samples were identical and the data were gathered at the same time. Florida also participated in the state survey, but its data collection was unavoidably delayed until 1993.

Finally, more than 1,100 inmates in some 80 federal and state prisons were included in the survey. Their participation helped to provide better estimates of the literacy levels of the total population and make it possible to report on the literacy proficiencies of this important segment of society. To ensure comparability with the national survey, the simulation tasks given to the prison participants were the same as those given to the household survey population. However, to address issues of particular relevance to the prison population, a revised version of the background questionnaire was developed. This instrument drew questions from the 1991 Survey of Inmates of State Correctional Facilities sponsored by the Bureau of Justice Statistics of the U.S. Department of Justice. These included queries about current offenses, criminal history, and prison work assignments, as well as about education and labor force experiences.

Responses from the national household, the state, and prison samples were combined to yield the best possible performance estimates. Unfortunately, because of the delayed administration, the results from the Florida state survey could not be included in the national estimates. In all, more than 26,000 adults gave, on average, more than an hour of their time to complete the literacy tasks and background questionnaires. Participants who completed as much of the assessment as their skills allowed were paid $20 for their time. The demographic characteristics of the adults who participated in NALS are presented in Table 1.

The National Adult Literacy Survey Sample

Total Population			
	Assessed Sample	National Population (in thousands)	Percentage of National Population
Total	26,091	191,289	100%
Sex			
Male	11,770	92,098	48
Female	14,279	98,901	52
Age			
16 to 18 years	1,237	10,424	5
19 to 24 years	3,344	24,515	13
25 to 39 years	10,050	63,278	33
40 to 54 years	6,310	43,794	23
55 to 64 years	2,924	19,503	10
65 years and older	2,214	29,735	16
Race/Ethnicity			
White	17,292	144,968	76
Black	4,963	21,192	11
Asian or Pacific Islander	438	4,116	2
American Indian or Alaskan Native	189	1,803	1
Other	83	729	0*
Hispanic/Mexican	1,776	10,235	5
Hispanic/Puerto Rican	405	2,190	1
Hispanic/Cuban	147	928	0*
Hispanic/Central or South American	424	2,608	1
Hispanic/Other	374	2,520	1

Prison Population			
	Assessed Sample	National Population (in thousands)	Percentage of National Population
Total	1,147	766	100%
Sex			
Male	1,076	723	94
Female	71	43	6
Race/Ethnicity			
White	417	266	35
Black	480	340	44
Asian or Pacific Islander	7	4	1
American Indian or Alaskan Native	27	18	2
Other	5	4	1
Hispanic groups	211	134	17

Notes: The total population includes adults living in households and those in prison. The sample sizes for subpopulations may not add up to the total sample sizes due to missing data. The race/ethnicity categories are mutually exclusive. Some estimates for small subgroups of the national population may be slightly different from 1990 Census estimates due to the sampling procedures used.

*Percentages below .5 are rounded to 0.

Source: U.S. Department of Education, National Center for Education Statistics, National Adult Literacy Survey, 1992.

356-371 0 - 93 - 2 : QL 3

Further information on the design of the sample, the survey administration, the statistical analyses and special studies that were conducted, and the validity of the literacy scales will be available in a forthcoming technical report, to be published in 1994.

Reporting the Results

The results of the National Adult Literacy Survey are reported using three scales, each ranging from 0 to 500: a prose scale, a document scale, and a quantitative scale. The scores on each scale represent degrees of proficiency along that particular dimension of literacy. For example, a low score (below 225) on the document scale indicates that an individual has very limited skills in processing information from tables, charts, graphs, maps, and the like (even those that are brief and uncomplicated). On the other hand, a high score (above 375) indicates advanced skills in performing a variety of tasks that involve the use of complex documents.

Survey participants received proficiency scores according to their performance on the survey tasks. A relatively small proportion of the respondents answered only a part of the survey, and an imputation procedure was used to make the best possible estimates of their proficiencies. This procedure and related issues are detailed in the technical report.

Most respondents tended to obtain similar, though not identical, scores on the three literacy scales. This does not mean, however, that the underlying skills involved in prose, document, and quantitative literacy are the same. Each scale provides some unique information, especially when comparisons are made across groups defined by variables such as race/ethnicity, education, and age.

The literacy scales allow us not only to summarize results for various subpopulations, but also to determine the relative difficulty of the literacy tasks included in the survey. In other words, just as individuals received scale scores according to their performance in the assessment, the literacy tasks received specific scale values according to their difficulty, as determined by the performance of the adults who participated in the survey. Previous research has shown that the difficulty of a literacy task, and therefore its placement on the literacy scale, is determined by three factors: the *structure of the material* — for example, exposition, narrative, table, graph, map, or advertisement; the *content* of the material and/or the *context* from which it is drawn — for example, home, work, or community; and the *nature of the task* — that is, what the individual is asked to do with the material, or his or her purpose for using it.[3]

The literacy tasks administered in NALS varied widely in terms of materials, content, and task requirements, and thus in terms of difficulty. This range is captured in Figure 1, which describes some of the literacy tasks and indicates their scale values.

Even a cursory review of this display reveals that tasks at the lower end of each scale differ from those at the high end. A more careful analysis of the range of tasks along each scale provides clear evidence of an ordered set of information-processing skills and strategies. On the prose scale, for example, tasks with low scale values ask readers to locate or identify information in brief, familiar, or uncomplicated materials, while those at the high end ask them to perform more demanding activities using materials that tend to be lengthy, unfamiliar, or complex. Similarly, on the document and quantitative scales, the tasks at the low end of the scale differ from those at the high end in terms of the structure of the material, the content and context of the material, and the nature of the directive.

In an attempt to capture this progression of information-processing skills and strategies, each scale was divided into five levels: *Level 1* (0 to 225), *Level 2* (226 to 275), *Level 3* (276 to 325), *Level 4* (326 to 375), and *Level 5* (376 to 500). The points and score ranges that separate these levels on each scale reflect shifts in the literacy skills and strategies required to perform increasingly complex tasks. The survey tasks were assigned to the appropriate point on the appropriate scale based on their difficulty as reflected in the performance of the nationally representative sample of adults surveyed. Analyses of the types of materials and demands that characterize each level reveal the progression of literacy demands along each scale (FIGURE 2).

While the literacy levels on each scale can be used to explore the range of literacy demands, these data do not reveal the types of literacy demands that are associated with particular contexts in this pluralistic society. That is, they do not enable us to say what specific level of prose, document, or quantitative skill is required to obtain, hold, or advance in a particular occupation, to manage a household, or to obtain legal or community services, for example. Nevertheless, the relationships among performance on the three scales and various social or economic indicators can provide valuable insights, and that is the goal of this report.

---

[3] I.S. Kirsch and P.B. Mosenthal. (1990). "Exploring Document Literacy: Variables Underlying the Performance of Young Adults," *Reading Research Quarterly*, 25. pp. 5-30. P.B. Mosenthal and I.S. Kirsch. (1992). "Defining the Constructs of Adult Literacy," paper presented at the National Reading Conference, San Antonio, Texas.

Difficulty Values of Selected Tasks Along the Prose, Document, and Quantitative Literacy Scales

Prose	Document	Quantitative
149 Identify country in short article	**69** Sign your name	**191** Total a bank deposit entry
210 Locate one piece of information in sports article	**170** Locate expiration date on driver's license	
224 Underline sentence explaining action stated in short article	**180** Locate time of meeting on a form	
	214 Using pie graph, locate type of vehicle having specific sales	
226 Underline meaning of a term given in government brochure on supplemental security income	**230** Locate intersection on a street map	**238** Calculate postage and fees for certified mail
250 Locate two features of information in sports article	**246** Locate eligibility from table of employee benefits	**246** Determine difference in price between tickets for two shows
275 Interpret instructions from an appliance warranty	**259** Identify and enter background information on application for social security card	**270** Calculate total costs of purchase from an order form
288 Write a brief letter explaining error made on a credit card bill	**277** Identify information from bar graph depicting source of energy and year	**278** Using calculator, calculate difference between regular and sale price from an advertisement
304 Read a news article and identify a sentence that provides interpretation of a situation	**298** Use sign out sheet to respond to call about resident	**308** Using calculator, determine the discount from an oil bill if paid within 10 days
316 Read lengthy article to identify two behaviors that meet a stated condition	**314** Use bus schedule to determine appropriate bus for given set of conditions	**321** Calculate miles per gallon using information given on mileage record chart
	323 Enter information given into an automobile maintenance record form	**325** Plan travel arrangements for meeting using flight schedule
328 State in writing an argument made in lengthy newspaper article	**342** Identify the correct percentage meeting specified conditions from a table of such information	**331** Determine correct change using information in a menu
347 Explain difference between two types of employee benefits	**352** Use bus schedule to determine appropriate bus for given set of conditions	**350** Using information stated in news article, calculate amount of money that should go to raising a child
359 Contrast views expressed in two editorials on technologies available to make fuel-efficient cars	**352** Use table of information to determine pattern in oil exports across years	**368** Using eligibility pamphlet, calculate the yearly amount a couple would receive for basic supplemental security income
362 Generate unfamiliar theme from short poems		
374 Compare two metaphors used in poem		
382 Compare approaches stated in narrative on growing up	**378** Use information in table to complete a graph including labeling axes	**382** Determine shipping and total costs on an order form for items in a catalog
410 Summarize two ways lawyers may challenge prospective jurors	**387** Use table comparing credit cards. Identify the two categories used and write two differences between them	**405** Using information in news article, calculate difference in times for completing a race
423 Interpret a brief phrase from a lengthy news article	**395** Using a table depicting information about parental involvement in school survey to write a paragraph summarizing extent to which parents and teachers agree	**421** Using calculator, determine the total cost of carpet to cover a room

Scale markers: 0, 225, 275, 325, 375, 500

Source: U.S. Department of Education, National Center for Education Statistics, National Adult Literacy Survey, 1992.

Description of the Prose, Document, and Quantitative Literacy Levels

	Prose	Document	Quantitative
Level 1 *0-225*	Most of the tasks in this level require the reader to read relatively short text to locate a single piece of information which is identical to or synonymous with the information given in the question or directive. If plausible but incorrect information is present in the text, it tends not to be located near the correct information.	Tasks in this level tend to require the reader either to locate a piece of information based on a literal match or to enter information from personal knowledge onto a document. Little, if any, distracting information is present.	Tasks in this level require readers to perform single, relatively simple arithmetic operations, such as addition. The numbers to be used are provided and the arithmetic operation to be performed is specified.
Level 2 *226-275*	Some tasks in this level require readers to locate a single piece of information in the text; however, several distractors or plausible but incorrect pieces of information may be present, or low-level inferences may be required. Other tasks require the reader to integrate two or more pieces of information or to compare and contrast easily identifiable information based on a criterion provided in the question or directive.	Tasks in this level are more varied than those in Level 1. Some require the readers to match a single piece of information; however, several distractors may be present, or the match may require low-level inferences. Tasks in this level may also ask the reader to cycle through information in a document or to integrate information from various parts of a document.	Tasks in this level typically require readers to perform a single operation using numbers that are either stated in the task or easily located in the material. The operation to be performed may be stated in the question or easily determined from the format of the material (for example, an order form).
Level 3 *276-325*	Tasks in this level tend to require readers to make literal or synonymous matches between the text and information given in the task, or to make matches that require low-level inferences. Other tasks ask readers to integrate information from dense or lengthy text that contains no organizational aids such as headings. Readers may also be asked to generate a response based on information that can be easily identified in the text. Distracting information is present, but is not located near the correct information.	Some tasks in this level require the reader to integrate multiple pieces of information from one or more documents. Others ask readers to cycle through rather complex tables or graphs which contain information that is irrelevant or inappropriate to the task.	In tasks in this level, two or more numbers are typically needed to solve the problem, and these must be found in the material. The operation(s) needed can be determined from the arithmetic relation terms used in the question or directive.
Level 4 *326-375*	These tasks require readers to perform multiple-feature matches and to integrate or synthesize information from complex or lengthy passages. More complex inferences are needed to perform successfully. Conditional information is frequently present in tasks at this level and must be taken into consideration by the reader.	Tasks in this level, like those at the previous levels, ask readers to perform multiple-feature matches, cycle through documents, and integrate information; however, they require a greater degree of inferencing. Many of these tasks require readers to provide numerous responses but do not designate how many responses are needed. Conditional information is also present in the document tasks at this level and must be taken into account by the reader.	These tasks tend to require readers to perform two or more sequential operations or a single operation in which the quantities are found in different types of displays, or the operations must be inferred from semantic information given or drawn from prior knowledge.
Level 5 *376-500*	Some tasks in this level require the reader to search for information in dense text which contains a number of plausible distractors. Others ask readers to make high-level inferences or use specialized background knowledge. Some tasks ask readers to contrast complex information.	Tasks in this level require the reader to search through complex displays that contain multiple distractors, to make high-level text-based inferences, and to use specialized knowledge.	These tasks require readers to perform multiple operations sequentially. They must disembed the features of the problem from text or rely on background knowledge to determine the quantities or operations needed.

Source: U.S. Department of Education, National Center for Education Statistics, National Adult Literacy Survey, 1992.

About This Report

This report is written in three sections. The next two sections present the results of the survey. Section I provides information on the distribution of literacy skills in the population as a whole and in an array of subgroups defined by level of education, age, race/ethnicity, country of birth, region of the country, and disability status. Section II explores how literacy levels relate to employment and earnings, poverty status, sources of income, voting behavior, and reading activities.

Section III describes the levels of literacy for each scale, providing contextual information that illuminates the proficiency results presented in the first and second sections. Sample tasks are reproduced to illustrate the characteristics of specific tasks as well as to show the range of performance demands on each scale. In addition, the knowledge and skills reflected in these tasks are analyzed.

In interpreting the results herein, readers should bear in mind that the literacy tasks contained in this assessment and the adults invited to participate in the survey are samples drawn from their two respective universes. As such, they are subject to some measurable degree of uncertainty. Scientific procedures employed in the study design and the scaling of literacy tasks permit a high degree of confidence in the resulting estimates of task difficulty. Similarly, the sampling design and weighting procedures applied in this survey assure that participants' responses can be generalized to the populations of interest.

In an effort to make this report as readable as possible, numbers throughout have been rounded and presented without standard errors (or estimates about their accuracy). Where differences between various subpopulations are discussed, the comparisons are based on statistical tests that consider the magnitude of the differences (for example, the difference in average document proficiency between high school and college graduates), the size of the standard errors associated with the numbers being compared, and the number of comparisons being made. Only statistically significant differences (at the .05 level) are discussed herein. Readers who are interested in making their own comparisons are therefore advised not to use the numbers alone to compare various groups, but rather to rely on statistical tests.[4]

Throughout this report, graphs are used to communicate the results to a broad audience, as well as to provide a source of informative displays which

---

[4] To determine whether the difference between two groups is statistically significant, one must estimate the degree of uncertainty (or the standard error) associated with the difference. To do so, one squares each group's standard error, sums these squared standard errors, then takes the square root of this sum. The difference between the two groups plus or minus twice the standard error of the difference is the confidence interval. If the confidence interval does not contain zero, then the difference between the two groups is said to be statistically significant.

policymakers and others may wish to use for their own purposes. More technical information is presented in the appendices at the end of the report.

The goal of this report is to provide useful information to all those who wish to understand the current status of literacy among America's adults and to strengthen existing adult literacy policies and programs. In considering the results, the reader should keep in mind that this was a survey of literacy in the English language — not literacy in any universal sense of the word. Thus, the results do not capture the literacy resources and abilities that some respondents possess in languages other than English.

A Note on Interpretations

In reviewing the information contained in this report, readers should be aware that no single factor determines what an individual's literacy proficiencies will be. All of us develop our own unique repertoire of competencies depending on a wide array of conditions and circumstances, including our family backgrounds, educational attainments, interests and aspirations, economic resources, and employment experiences. Any single survey, this one included, can focus on only some of these variables.

Further, while the survey results reveal certain characteristics that are related to literacy, the nature of the survey makes it impossible to determine the direction of these relationships. In other words, it is impossible to identify the extent to which literacy shapes particular aspects of our lives or is, in turn, shaped by them. For example, there is a strong relationship between educational attainment and literacy proficiencies. On the one hand, it is likely that staying in school longer does strengthen an individual's literacy skills. On the other hand, it is also true that those with more advanced skills tend to remain in school longer. Other variables, as well, are likely to play a role in the relationship between literacy and education. In interpreting such relationships in this report, the authors strive to acknowledge the many factors involved.

A final note deserves emphasis. This report describes the literacy proficiencies of various subpopulations defined by characteristics such as age, sex, race, ethnicity, and educational background. While certain groups demonstrated lower literacy skills than others on average, within every group there were some individuals who performed well and some who performed poorly. Accordingly, when one group is said to have lower average proficiencies than another, this does not imply that all adults in the first group performed worse than those in the second. Such statements are only intended to highlight general patterns of differences among various groups and therefore do not capture the variability within each group.

SECTION I

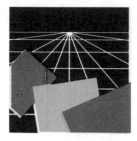

SECTION I

The Prose, Document, and Quantitative Literacies of America's Adults

The National Adult Literacy Survey gathered information on multiple dimensions of adult literacy. This section of the report profiles the prose, document, and quantitative literacy skills of the adult population and examines the complex relationships between literacy proficiencies and various demographic and background characteristics. For example, we compare the literacy proficiencies that adults demonstrated in this assessment with their self-reported evaluations of their reading and writing skills in English. Performance results are also reported for adults in terms of their level of educational attainment, age, race/ethnicity, region, and sex. The literacy skills of the total adult population and the prison population are compared, and the results for various racial/ethnic groups are described with respect to age, country of birth, and education.[1]

The results of the National Adult Literacy Survey are examined in two ways. General comparisons of literacy proficiency are made by examining the average performance of various subpopulations on each of the literacy scales. This information is interesting in and of itself, but it says little about how literacy is distributed among America's adults. To explore the range of literacy skills in the total population and in various subpopulations, the percentages of adults who performed in each level on the prose, document, and quantitative literacy scales are also presented. As described in the Introduction, five literacy levels were defined along each of the scales: *Level 1* (ranging from 0 to 225), *Level 2* (226 to 275), *Level 3* (276 to 325), *Level 4* (326 to 375), and *Level 5* (376 to 500).[2]

Because each literacy level encompasses a range on a given scale, the tasks in any particular level are not homogeneous, and neither are the individuals who performed in that level. Tasks in the high end of the range for a given level

---

[1] All subpopulations and variables discussed in this report are defined in the appendices.

[2] An overview of the literacy levels on each scale is provided in the Introduction. Section III describes the levels in more detail and includes examples of the types of tasks that were likely to be performed successfully by individuals in each level.

are more challenging than those in the low end, just as individuals whose proficiencies are in the high end of a level demonstrated success on a more challenging set of literacy tasks than individuals in the low end. The group of adults in Level 1 is especially heterogeneous, as it includes individuals who successfully performed only the relatively undemanding literacy tasks, those who attempted to perform these tasks but did not succeed, and those with such limited skills (or such limited English proficiency) that they did not try to respond at all. Thus, while the literacy levels are discussed as distinct units in this section, the heterogeneity of performance within each level should be kept in mind.

Results for the Total Population

Twenty-one percent of adults performed in Level 1 on the prose scale, while 23 percent performed in this level on the document scale and 22 percent were in this level on the quantitative scale (FIGURE 1.1). Translated into population terms, between 40 and 44 million adults nationwide demonstrated skills in the lowest literacy level defined.

What do these results mean? As noted earlier, there was a range of performance within Level 1. Some individuals in this level displayed the ability to read relatively short pieces of text to find a single piece of information. Some were able to enter personal information, such as their name, onto a document, or to locate the time of an event on a form. Some were able to add numbers on a bank deposit slip, or to perform other simple arithmetic operations using numbers presented to them. Other adults in Level 1, however, did not demonstrate the ability to perform even these fairly common and uncomplicated literacy tasks. There were individuals who had such limited skills that they were able to complete only part of the survey, and others who attempted to perform the literacy tasks they were given and were unsuccessful.

To understand these results, it is helpful to examine the characteristics of adults who demonstrated performance in Level 1. On the prose scale, for example, approximately one-quarter of the individuals who performed in this level reported that they were born in another country, and some of them were undoubtedly recent immigrants with a limited command of English (TABLE 1.1). In addition, 62 percent of the individuals in Level 1 on the prose scale said they had not completed high school; 35 percent, in fact, had finished no more than 8 years of schooling. Relatively high percentages of the respondents in this level were Black, Hispanic, or Asian/Pacific Islander, and many — approximately 33 percent — were age 65 or older. Further, 26 percent of the adults who performed in Level 1 said they had a physical, mental, or health condition that

Literacy Levels and Average Literacy Proficiencies for the Total Population

PROSE

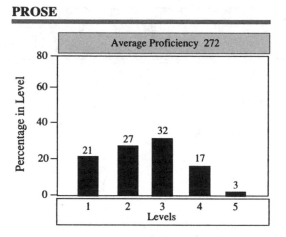

DOCUMENT

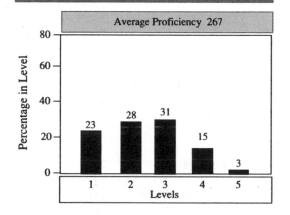

QUANTITATIVE

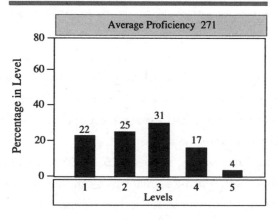

Level 1 (0 to 225)   **Level 2** (226 to 275)   **Level 3** (276 to 325)   **Level 4** (326 to 375)   **Level 5** (376 to 500)

Source: U.S. Department of Education, National Center for Education Statistics, National Adult Literacy Survey, 1992.

**Percentages of Adults with Selected Characteristics, Prose Level 1
and Total Populations**

	Prose Level 1 Population	Total Population
Country of Birth		
Born in another country or territory	25	10
Highest Level of Education Completed		
0 to 8 years	35	10
9 to 12 years	27	13
High school diploma	21	27
GED	3	4
Race/Ethnicity		
White	51	76
Black	20	11
Hispanic	23	10
Asian/Pacific Islander	4	2
Age		
16 to 24 years	13	18
65 years and older	33	16
Disability or Condition		
Any physical, mental, or health condition	26	12
Visual difficulty	19	7
Hearing difficulty	13	7
Learning disability	9	3

Source: U.S. Department of Education, National Center for Education Statistics, National Adult Literacy Survey, 1992.

kept them from participating fully in work and other activities, and 19 percent reported having vision problems that made it difficult for them to read print. In sum, the individuals in Level 1 had a diverse set of characteristics that influenced their performance in the assessment.

Across the three literacy scales, between 25 and 28 percent of the individuals surveyed — representing as many as 54 million adults nationwide — performed in Level 2. On the prose scale, those whose proficiencies lie within the range for this level demonstrated the ability to make low-level inferences based on what they read and to compare or contrast information that can easily be found in text. Individuals in Level 2 on the document scale were generally able to locate a piece of information in a document in which plausible but incorrect information was also present. Individuals in Level 2 on the quantitative scale were likely to give correct responses to a task involving a single arithmetic operation using numbers that can easily be located in printed material.

Nearly one-third of the respondents, representing some 61 million adults across the country, performed in Level 3 on each of the literacy scales. Those in this level on the prose scale demonstrated the ability to match pieces of information by making low-level inferences and to integrate information from relatively long or dense text. Those in the third level on the document scale were generally able to integrate multiple pieces of information found in documents. Adults in Level 3 on the quantitative scale demonstrated the ability to perform arithmetic operations by using two or more numbers found in printed material and by interpreting arithmetic terms included in the question.

Seventeen percent of the adults performed in Level 4 on the prose and quantitative scales, while 15 percent were in this level on the document scale. These respondents, who completed many of the more difficult assessment tasks successfully, represent from 29 to almost 33 million individuals nationwide. Looking across the scales, adults in Level 4 displayed an ability to synthesize information from lengthy or complex passages, to make inferences based on text and documents, and to perform sequential arithmetic operations using numbers found in different types of displays. To give correct responses to these types of tasks, readers were often required to make high level text-based inferences or to draw on their background knowledge.

Only 3 percent of the respondents performed in Level 5 on the prose and document scales, and 4 percent performed in this level on the quantitative scale. Some tasks at this level required readers to contrast complex information found in written materials, while others required them to make high level inferences or to search for information in dense text. On the document scale, adults performing in Level 5 showed the ability to use specialized knowledge and to search through complex displays for particular pieces of information. Respondents in the highest level on the quantitative scale demonstrated the ability to determine the features of arithmetic problems either by examining text or by using background knowledge, and then to perform the multiple arithmetic operations required. Between 6 and 8 million adults nationwide demonstrated success on these types of tasks — the most difficult of those included in the survey.

One of the questions that arises from these data is whether people with restricted skills perceived themselves as having inadequate or limited English literacy proficiency. To address this question, we identified the percentages of individuals in each level on the scales who responded "not well" or "not at all" to the questions, "How well do you read English?" and "How well do you write English?" (TABLE 1.2)

Table 1.2

Percentages of Adults Who Reported Not Being Able to Read or Write English Well, by Literacy Level

	Total Population	Level 1	Level 2	Level 3	Level 4	Level 5
Reading						
Prose	7	29	3	1	0*	0*
Document	7	25	3	1	0*	0*
Quantitative	7	26	3	1	0*	0*
Writing						
Prose	10	34	6	2	1	0*
Document	10	30	6	3	1	0*
Quantitative	10	30	7	3	1	0*

*Percentages below .5 are rounded to 0.

Source: U.S. Department of Education, National Center for Education Statistics, National Adult Literacy Survey, 1992.

When these self-reported evaluations of English literacy are compared with the data on actual performance, an interesting contrast appears. Of the 40 to 44 million adults who performed in Level 1 on the prose scale (as shown in Figure 1.1), only 29 percent said they did not read English well and 34 percent said they did not write English well. Similarly, on the document scale, 25 percent of the adults who performed in Level 1 reported having limited reading skills and 30 percent reported having limited writing skills. On the quantitative scale, 26 percent of the respondents in Level 1 reported not being able to read well and 30 percent said they did not write well.

The gap between performance and perception continues in Level 2. On each scale, only 3 to 7 percent of the individuals in this level said they did not read or write English well. These data indicate that the overwhelming majority of adults who demonstrated low levels of literacy did not perceive that they had a problem with respect to reading or writing in English. Such a mismatch may well have a significant impact on efforts to provide education and training to adults: Those who do not believe they have a problem will be less likely to seek out such services or less willing to take advantage of services that might be available to them.

Another way to determine how adults view their ability to read and write in English is to ask how often they receive help from others in performing everyday prose, document, and quantitative literacy tasks. Such questions were included in the survey, and the responses indicate that individuals who performed in the Level 1 range on each scale were far more likely than those in the higher levels to say that they get a lot of assistance with everyday literacy tasks (TABLE 1.3). Specifically, individuals in the lowest level of prose literacy were more likely than those in the higher levels to get a lot of help in reading printed information; adults in the lowest level of document literacy were more likely to get a lot of assistance in filling out forms; and adults in the lowest level of quantitative literacy were more likely to get a lot of help in using basic arithmetic.

Overall, 9 percent of the adults surveyed said they get a lot of help from family members or friends with printed information associated with government agencies, public companies, private businesses, hospitals, and so on. Yet, a much higher percentage of respondents in Level 1 on the prose scale — 23 percent — reported getting a lot of help with these types of materials. Relatively small proportions of the adults in the other literacy levels said they receive assistance with everyday prose tasks.

NALS _____ Table 1.3

Percentages of Adults Who Reported Getting A Lot of Help from Family Members or Friends With Various Types of Everyday Literacy Tasks, by Literacy Level

	Total Population	Level 1	Level 2	Level 3	Level 4	Level 5
Prose tasks: printed information	9	23	8	5	2	1
Document tasks: filling out forms	12	25	12	7	4	2
Quantitative tasks: using basic arithmetic	5	14	4	2	1	0*

*Percentages below .5 are rounded to 0.

Note: The first row presents responses for adults in each level of *prose* literacy; the second row presents responses for adults in each level of *document* literacy; and the third row presents responses for adults in each level of *quantitative* literacy.

Source: U.S. Department of Education, National Center for Education Statistics, National Adult Literacy Survey, 1992.

Twelve percent of the total population reported getting a lot of help from family members or friends with filling out forms. Again, however, those in the lowest level of document literacy were far more likely than those in the higher levels to report getting a lot of help with these types of everyday document tasks. One-quarter of those in Level 1, 12 percent of those in Level 2, and smaller percentages of those in the higher levels said they get a lot of help with forms.

Just 5 percent of the total adult population reported getting a lot of assistance in using basic arithmetic when filling out order forms or balancing a checkbook. Yet, a much higher percentage of adults in Level 1 on the quantitative scale — 14 percent — said they receive a lot of help from family and friends on these types of quantitative tasks. Smaller proportions of adults in Levels 2 through 5 on this scale reported getting a lot of help from others in using basic arithmetic.

Two patterns are apparent in the responses to these questions. First, individuals in Level 1 on each scale were considerably more likely than those in the higher proficiency levels to say they get a lot of help from family or friends with prose, document, and quantitative literacy tasks encountered in everyday life. Second, the proportions of adults in Level 1 on each scale who said they get a lot of help with these types of tasks are lower than might be expected. Across the scales, just 14 to 25 percent of the respondents in the lowest literacy level reported getting a lot of help reading printed information, filling out forms, and using basic arithmetic.

Taken together, the data in Tables 1.1 and 1.2 indicate that most adults who performed in the lowest level on each literacy scale believed they read and write English well, and most reportedly did not get a lot of assistance from friends or family with everyday literacy tasks. Of the 40 to 44 million adults who demonstrated the most limited skills, only about 14 million or fewer said they do not read or write English well, and as few as 6 million said they get a lot of assistance with everyday prose, document, and quantitative literacy tasks.

Trends in the Literacy Skills of Young Adults

In examining the literacy proficiencies of the adult population, one of the questions that naturally arises is whether skills are improving or slipping over time. Using the NALS data, this question can be addressed by comparing the performance of 21- to 25-year-olds assessed in 1985 first with young adults in the same age group who were assessed in 1992, and second with 28- to 32-year-olds assessed in 1992, who were 21 to 25 years old in 1985. These comparisons are possible because the same definition of literacy was used in this survey and the young adult survey and because a common set of prose, document, and quantitative literacy tasks was administered in both assessments.

Since the earlier study assessed the skills of individuals aged 21 to 25 who were living in households, the NALS data were reanalyzed to determine the proficiencies of adults in the 21 to 25 age group and those in the 28 to 32 age group who were living in households at the time of the 1992 survey. Adults in prison were excluded from the analyses to make the samples more comparable.[3]

These comparisons reveal that the average prose, document, and quantitative proficiencies of America's young adults were somewhat lower in 1992 than they were seven years earlier (FIGURE 1.2). While 21- to 25-year-olds assessed in 1985 demonstrated average proficiencies of about 293 on each of the literacy scales, the scores of 21- to 25-year-olds assessed in 1992 were 11 to 14 points lower: 281 on the prose and document scales and 279 on the quantitative scale. The average proficiencies of adults aged 28 to 32 who participated in the 1992 survey were also lower than those of 21- to 25-year-olds in the earlier survey, by 10 to 11 points across the three scales.

Many factors may be involved, but the discrepancies in literacy performance between the 1985 and 1992 respondents can be explained at least in part by changes in the composition of the young adult population. While the proportions of young Black adults changed little from one survey to the next (13 percent to 11 percent), and the percentages of White adults decreased (from 76 to 70 percent), the percentages of young Hispanic adults doubled, rising from 7 percent of the 1985 survey participants to 15 percent of the 21- to 25-year-old NALS participants. Many of these Hispanic individuals were born in other countries and are learning English as a second language.

When one examines the trends in literacy proficiencies within various racial or ethnic groups, different patterns are visible.[4] Among White adults, those aged 21 to 25 who were assessed in 1992 demonstrated lower average proficiencies than adults in this same age group who participated in the 1985 survey. Performance declined from 305 to 296 on both the prose and document scales, and from 304 to 295 on the quantitative scale. In contrast, the average prose, document, and quantitative proficiencies of 28- to 32-year-olds assessed in 1992 were not significantly different from those of adults aged 21 to 25 who were assessed in 1985.

---

[3] To further enhance the comparability of the 1985 and 1992 survey results, the 1985 data were reanalyzed using the same statistical procedures that were used in NALS. For example, respondents who completed only part of the survey were eliminated from the 1985 analyses but were included in the analyses for the current study. As a result of such adjustments, the 1985 survey results reported here are slightly different from those in previous reports. These issues and procedures are to be discussed in the technical report.

[4] Trends in the performance of White, Black, and Hispanic adults are discussed here; the numbers of Asian/Pacific Islanders who participated in the 1985 survey were too small to permit reliable comparisons across the two surveys.

Figure 1.2

Average Literacy Proficiencies of Young Adults, 1985 and 1992

PROSE

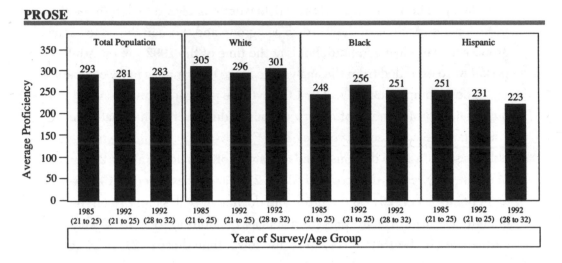

DOCUMENT

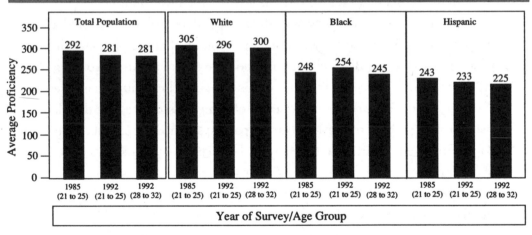

QUANTITATIVE

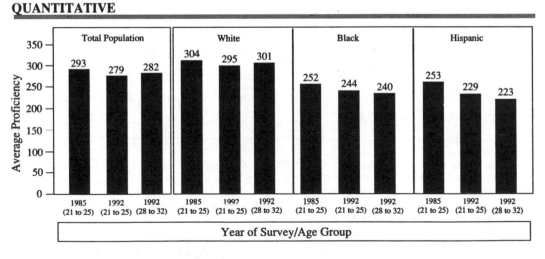

Source: U.S. Department of Education, National Center for Education Statistics, National Adult Literacy Survey, 1992.

The pattern for Black individuals is somewhat different. The average prose, document, and quantitative proficiencies of 21- to 25-year-old Black adults assessed in 1992 were comparable to those of young Black adults assessed in 1985. Black NALS participants in the 28 to 32 age group demonstrated similar prose and document proficiencies but lower quantitative scores (240 compared with 252) than participants in the young adult survey.

When the literacy skills of young Hispanic adults assessed in 1985 are compared with the skills of those assessed in 1992, still a different pattern is seen. Hispanic adults aged 21 to 25 who participated in the earlier assessment demonstrated an average prose score of 251, an average document score of 243, and an average quantitative score of 253. Their same-age peers who participated in the 1992 assessment demonstrated quantitative proficiencies that were 24 points lower. While their average prose and document scores were also lower, the 10- to 20-point differences did not reach statistical significance. Hispanic adults aged 28 to 32 who participated in the 1992 survey demonstrated lower average prose and quantitative proficiencies than young Hispanic adults who participated in the 1985 survey. The proficiency gap on the prose scale was 28 points, while on the quantitative scale, it was 30 points. Although large, the 18-point difference on the document scale did not reach statistical significance. Again, these performance differences between the 1985 and 1992 surveys can be explained, at least in part, by demographic changes in the young adult population over the seven-year period.

Results by Level of Education

A primary means of transmitting literacy to succeeding generations is the school system. Not surprisingly, then, among all the variables explored in the survey, the level of education attained in the United States has the strongest relationship with demonstrated literacy proficiency (FIGURE 1.3). Adults with higher levels of education demonstrated much higher average proficiencies than those with fewer years of schooling. As previously observed, however, the relationship between schooling and literacy is complex. Schooling surely increases an individual's skills, but it is also true that individuals with higher proficiencies are more likely to extend their schooling.

What is most interesting is the steady rise in average literacy proficiencies across the entire range of education levels. (Throughout this section, "level of education" refers to the highest level of education that respondents reported having completed at the time of the survey.) The average prose proficiency of adults who did not go beyond eighth grade was 177, compared with 270 for those who completed high school but went no further, 322 for those whose

Figure 1.3

Literacy Levels and Average Literacy Proficiencies, by Highest Level of Education Completed

PROSE

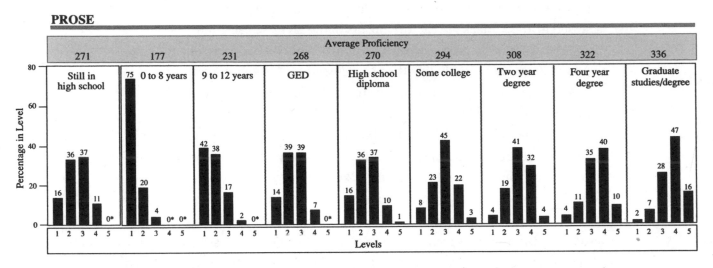

DOCUMENT

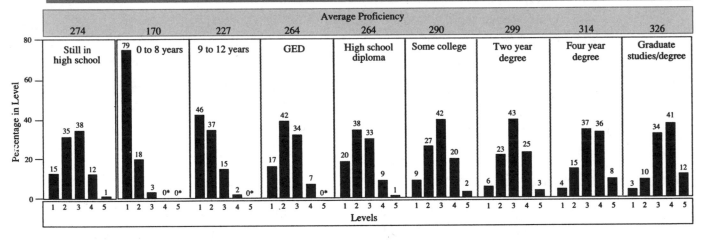

QUANTITATIVE

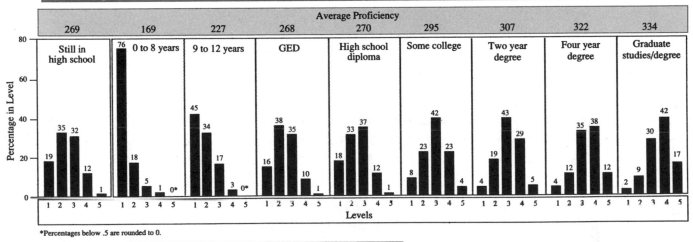

*Percentages below .5 are rounded to 0.

Level 1 (0 to 225) **Level 2** (226 to 275) **Level 3** (276 to 325) **Level 4** (326 to 375) **Level 5** (376 to 500)

Source: U.S. Department of Education, National Center for Education Statistics, National Adult Literacy Survey, 1992.

highest level of education was a four-year college degree, and 336 for those who had completed some graduate studies beyond the four-year degree. Similar patterns are evident on the document and quantitative scales, where those with higher levels of education also displayed more advanced literacy skills.

Stated another way, the difference in average prose proficiencies between those who completed no more than 8 years of education and those who had completed at least some graduate work is nearly 160 points. This translates to a gap of roughly three proficiency levels, representing, on average, a very large difference in literacy skills and strategies. This may mean the difference, for example, between being able to identify a piece of information in a short news article and being able to compare and contrast information in lengthy text. While adults with less than a high school education performed primarily in Level 1, those who finished secondary school performed, on average, in the high end of Level 2, those who received a college degree demonstrated average proficiencies associated with the high end of Level 3, and those who had completed some work beyond the four-year degree performed within the range of Level 4.

On the whole, the performance of high school graduates was not as strong as might be desired. On each scale, between 16 and 20 percent of adults with high school diplomas performed in Level 1, and between 33 and 38 percent performed in Level 2. Conversely, only 10 to 13 percent of high school graduates reached the two highest levels. As expected, the performance of adults with General Educational Development (GED) certificates was nearly identical to that of adults with high school diplomas. The average proficiencies and the distributions across the literacy levels were highly similar for these two groups.

Large percentages of four-year college graduates reached the higher levels on each of the literacy scales. Fifty percent were in Levels 4 or 5 on the prose and quantitative scales, while 44 percent reached those levels on the document scale. Still, the percentages who performed in the two lowest levels are quite large: 15 percent on the prose scale, 19 percent on the document scale, and 16 percent on the quantitative scale.

The relationship between education and literacy will be further explored in an upcoming special report.

Results by Parents' Level of Education

The differences in literacy proficiencies among various groups are the result of many factors, some of which can be controlled by individuals and some of which cannot. Previous work investigating the intergenerational nature of literacy has revealed the major role that parents' economic status and educational attainment play in their children's success in school. Accordingly, adults participating in the NALS were asked to indicate the highest level of education that each of their parents had completed, and the highest level of education attained by either parent was used in these analyses.

Given that parents' education is a proxy for socioeconomic status, interests, and aspirations, one would expect to find that adults whose parents completed more years of education demonstrate more advanced literacy skills than those whose parents have limited education. This pattern is, in fact, evident in the NALS results. Individuals who reported that their parents earned college degrees demonstrated higher prose, document, and quantitative proficiency scores, on average, than those whose parents had not continued this far in their education. On the prose scale, for example, adults whose parents completed a college degree had an average score of 305, while those whose parents had not finished high school had an average proficiency of 264.

The important role of parents' education in the literacy skills of their offspring is underscored when the data on respondents' educational attainment are viewed as a function of their parents' educational attainment. For example, adults with high school diplomas had an average prose score of 255 if their parents completed 0 to 8 years of education; 267 if their parents attended high school but did not receive a diploma; 275 if their parents graduated from high school; and 286 if their parents earned a four-year degree (FIGURE 1.4). These trends are similar for each scale and each level of educational attainment, although not all comparisons are statistically significant.

While parents' education is clearly related to adults' proficiencies, the relationship between literacy proficiency and respondents' own level of education is even stronger. Within each category of parental education, adults who had completed more years of education demonstrated higher average proficiencies than those who had completed fewer years. For example, among individuals whose parents had completed no more than eight years of education, those who had attended high school but did not earn a diploma outperformed those with 0 to 8 years of education; the average prose proficiencies of these two groups were 218 and 174, respectively. Adults who completed high school attained an average prose score of 255, while those who earned a four-year college degree had an average score of 296.

Average Literacy Proficiencies, by Level of Education Attained by Adults and Their Parents

PROSE

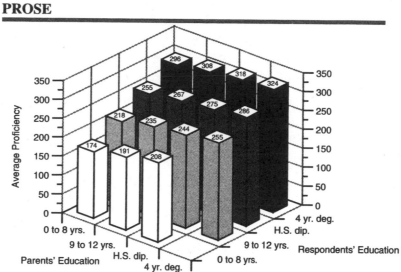

DOCUMENT

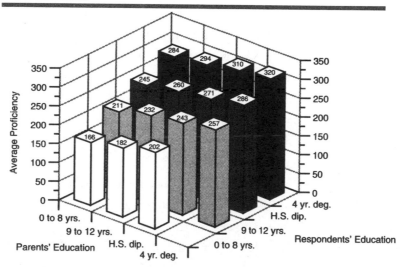

QUANTITATIVE

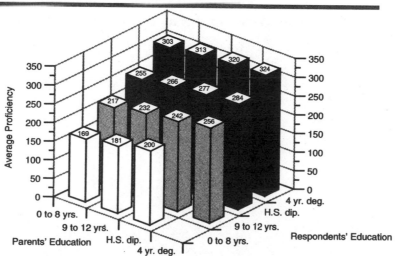

Notes: This figure presents results for only part of the population: those adults who represent a range of educational attainments. The numbers of adults with 0 to 8 years of education whose parents had a four year degree are too small to provide reliable proficiency estimates.

Source: U.S. Department of Education, National Center for Education Statistics, National Adult Literacy Survey, 1992.

Results by Age

The variations in performance across the age groups are highly similar for the prose and quantitative scales. On both of these scales, average scores increased from the teenage years up to the middle forties, with the largest increase occurring between 16- to 18-year-olds and 19- to 24-year-olds (FIGURE 1.5). Average proficiencies then declined sharply, falling approximately 25 points between the 40 to 54 age group and the 55 to 64 age group, and another 30 points or so between that group and the oldest adults.

On the document scale, the performance of the first four age groups (16 to 18, 19 to 24, 25 to 39, and 40 to 54) seems to be more similar than is the case on the prose and quantitative scales. Again, however, there are sharp declines in performance between adults aged 40 to 54 and those aged 55 to 64, and then for individuals 65 years and older. These decreases are 29 and 32 points, respectively, while the largest difference among the younger four age groups is 6 points.

To understand these declines in performance, it is helpful to compare the educational attainments of adults in the various age groups. These data clearly show that older adults (that is, individuals between the ages of 55 and 64 and those 65 and older) completed fewer years of schooling, on average, than did adults in the younger age groups (TABLE 1.4). The one exception is for 16- to 18-year-olds, many of whom are still in school.

The differences across the age groups in years of schooling parallel the differences in literacy proficiencies. Just as average performance declines among adults in the two oldest age groups, so too do the average years of schooling. Thus, it appears that some of the decrease in literacy skills across the age cohorts can be attributed to fewer years of schooling. Different immigration patterns may also help to explain the decline, as may other factors not examined in this survey. These patterns and relationships will be explored more fully in forthcoming reports on literacy among older adults and on literacy and education.

Average Literacy Proficiencies, by Age

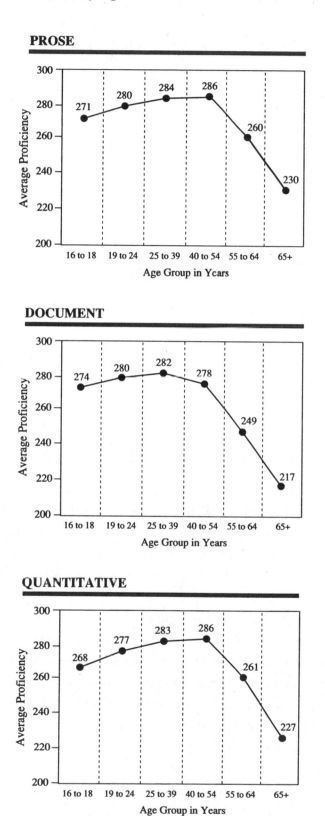

PROSE

DOCUMENT

QUANTITATIVE

Source: U.S. Department of Education, National Center for Education Statistics, National Adult Literacy Survey, 1992.

Average Years of Schooling, by Age

Age	Average Years of Schooling*
16 to 18 years**	10.8
19 to 24 years**	12.5
25 to 39 years	12.9
40 to 54 years	13.1
55 to 64 years	11.8
65 years and older	10.7

*in this country.
**Many adults in these age groups are still in school.

Source: U.S. Department of Education, National Center for Education Statistics, National Adult Literacy Survey, 1992.

Results by Race/Ethnicity

Because such a large number of adults participated in this survey, it is possible to report performance results for many more racial/ethnic groups than has been possible in the past.

The average prose literacy of White adults is 26 to 80 points higher than that of any of the other nine racial/ethnic groups reported here (FIGURE 1.6). Similar patterns are evident on the document and quantitative scales. On the document scale, the average scores of White adults are between 26 and 75 points higher than those of other groups, while on quantitative scale they are from 31 to 84 points higher.

With the exception of Hispanic/Other adults, the average proficiencies of the Hispanic subpopulations are not significantly different from one another. On average, Mexican and Central/South American adults were outperformed by Black adults. In contrast, Hispanic/Other adults outperformed Black adults on the prose and document scales by more than 20 points. (On the quantitative scale, the difference is not significant.) Their performance was, on average, similar to that of Asian/Pacific Islander adults and American Indian/Alaskan Native adults.

Literacy Levels and Average Literacy Proficiencies, by Race/Ethnicity

PROSE

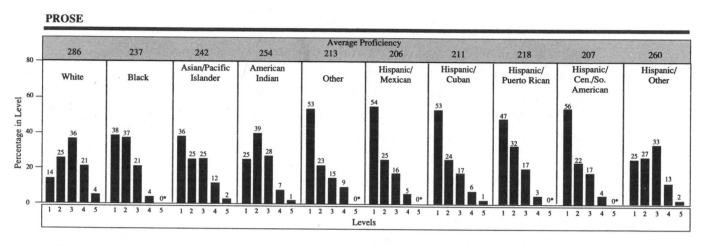

DOCUMENT

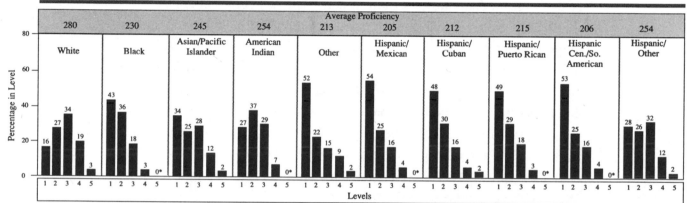

QUANTITATIVE

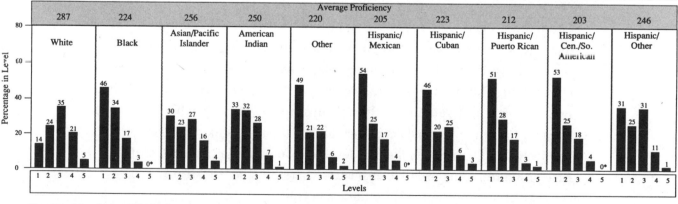

*Percentages below .5 are rounded to 0.

Level 1 (0 to 225)   **Level 2** (226 to 275)   **Level 3** (276 to 325)   **Level 4** (326 to 375)   **Level 5** (376 to 500)

Source: U.S. Department of Education, National Center for Education Statistics, National Adult Literacy Survey, 1992.

When one compares the average proficiency results for White and Black adults and for White and Asian/Pacific Islander adults, one sees very different patterns across the three literacy scales. While the proficiency gap between White and Black adults *increases* across the prose, document, and quantitative scales (from 49 to 63 points), the gap between White and Asian/Pacific Islander adults *decreases* (from 44 to 31 points). On the prose scale, the average proficiencies of White and Black adults differ by 49 points, compared with a difference of 44 points between White and Asian/Pacific Islander adults. On the document scale, the proficiency gap between White and Black adults is 50 points, whereas between White and Asian/Pacific Islander adults it is 35 points. On the quantitative scale, the average proficiency of White adults is 63 points higher than that of Black adults, but only 31 points higher than that of Asian/Pacific Islander adults.

The differences in average performance between Black and Asian/Pacific Islander respondents are even more striking. The two groups performed similarly on the prose and document scales, but Asian/Pacific Islander adults outperformed Black adults by 32 points on the quantitative scale. Such differences in the patterns of performance reflect the different backgrounds and experiences of these adults. If performance were reported on a single literacy scale, such important variations across the scales would be masked.

The racial/ethnic differences in performance reflect the influence of many variables. Data on some of these variables were collected as part of the National Adult Literacy Survey, including information on educational attainment, age, and country of birth.

Educational Attainment and Racial/Ethnic Differences

Given the strength of the relationship between adults' level of education and their literacy performance, it was hypothesized that proficiency differences among the various racial/ethnic groups might be related to varying educational attainments. The average years of schooling in this country reported by respondents in different racial/ethnic groups are presented in Table 1.5. Because the numbers of adults in each of the Hispanic subpopulations are relatively small, analyses of the nine levels of educational attainment within each group result in unreliable estimates. Therefore, the five Hispanic subpopulations are combined for these analyses.

Hispanic adults reported having had the fewest years of schooling of all the groups — just over 10 years, on average. The average years of education attained by Black adults and respondents of American Indian/Alaskan Native origin are similar: 11.6 and 11.7 years, respectively. Thus, these groups had

Average Years of Schooling, by Race/Ethnicity

Race/Ethnicity	Average Years of Schooling*
White	12.8
Black	11.6
Asian or Pacific Islander	13.0
American Indian or Alaskan Native	11.7
Hispanic groups	10.2

*in this country.

Source: U.S. Department of Education, National Center for Education Statistics, National Adult Literacy Survey, 1992.

completed more years of school than Hispanic adults, on average, but at least a year less than either White or Asian/Pacific Islander adults.

While these differences in years of education may help explain some of the gaps in performance among the various racial/ethnic groups, they do not explain all of the disparities that are found. Another way to examine the relationship between years of schooling and racial/ethnic differences is to compare proficiencies across levels of educational attainment (FIGURE 1.7).

For the most part, differences in average proficiencies among minority subgroups are reduced when comparisons are made only among individuals with the same levels of education. Even when one controls for level of education, however, large differences in average performance continue to be observed (TABLE 1.6).

The average differences in prose, document, and quantitative proficiencies between White and Black adults are 49, 50, and 63 points, respectively. When level of education is taken into account, the average proficiency differences across the nine levels of education decrease to 36, 37, and 48 points, respectively. The remaining disparities in performance between White and Black adults may be the result of numerous factors. One plausible explanation is the variation in the quality of education available to these two populations. Differences in socioeconomic status are also likely to be a factor.

When comparing the differences between White and Hispanic adults, the effects of controlling for education are even greater than for White and Black adults. This reflects the larger difference between these two groups in years of

Figure 1.7

Average Literacy Proficiencies, by Highest Level of Education Completed and Race/Ethnicity

PROSE

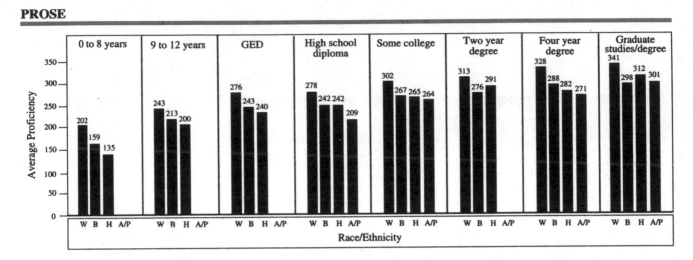

DOCUMENT

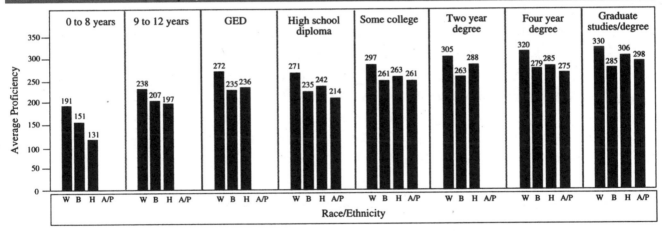

QUANTITATIVE

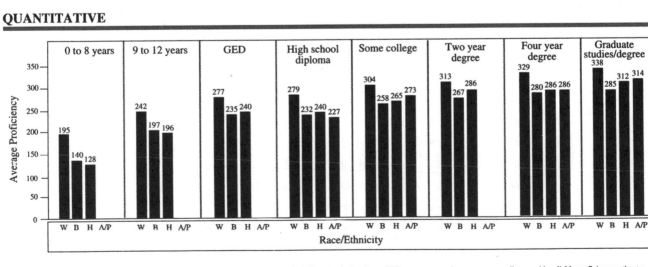

Note: The numbers of Asian/Pacific Islander adults who had completed 0 to 8 years or 9 to 12 years of education, a GED, or a two year degree are too small to provide reliable proficiency estimates.

W: White   B: Black   H: Hispanic groups   A/P: Asian/Pacific Islander

Source: U.S. Department of Education, National Center for Education Statistics, National Adult Literacy Survey, 1992.

Differences in Average Literacy Proficiencies Between Various Racial/Ethnic Groups, Overall and by Level of Education

Differences Between:	Overall Difference	Average Difference by Level of Education*
White and Black Adults		
Prose	49	36
Document	50	37
Quantitative	63	48
White and Hispanic Adults		
Prose	71	40
Document	67	35
Quantitative	75	41
White and Asian/Pacific Islander Adults		
Prose	44	54
Document	35	45
Quantitative	31	40

*The "average difference" column reflects the weighted average of the proficiency differences between each pair of groups across the levels of education. For the White-Black and White-Hispanic comparisons, the average is based on all nine levels of education. For the White-Asian/Pacific Islander comparisons, the average is based on the four levels of education for which there are reliable estimates.

Source: U.S. Department of Education, National Center for Education Statistics, National Adult Literacy Survey, 1992.

schooling, as reported in Table 1.5. The average difference across the three scales is reduced by almost 50 percent when level of education is taken into consideration. Overall, the average differences in prose, document, and quantitative proficiencies between White and Hispanic adults are 71, 67, and 75 points, respectively. When one takes levels of education into account, however, these differences decline to 40, 35, and 41 points across the three literacy scales.

In contrast, given the similarity in the number of years of schooling completed by White and Asian/Pacific Islander adults, the differences in average performance do not change significantly when level of education is taken into account. That is, whereas the average differences in prose, document, and quantitative performance between White adults and respondents of Asian/Pacific Islander origin are 44, 35, and 31 points, respectively, the average differences are 54, 45, and 40 points on the three scales when one compares performance while controlling for level of education.

356-371 0 - 93 - 3 : QL 3

While there continue to be disparities in educational attainment among individuals with different racial/ethnic characteristics, levels of education have risen for all individuals throughout the last century. Therefore, it seems important to explore racial/ethnic group differences in various age cohorts. One might expect that the differences in average years of education among the racial/ethnic groups would be smaller for younger adults, and that the differences in average proficiencies would therefore be higher for older adults.

Figure 1.8 shows the differences in average literacy proficiencies and in average years of schooling between White adults and those in the other minority groups by age. The differences in average years of schooling between White and Black adults and between White and Hispanic adults increase across the age groups, and so it is not surprising to see that these are mirrored by rising disparities in literacy performance. For example, across the scales, the average proficiency difference between Black and White adults in the 16 to 18 age group is 36 to 47 points. The accompanying difference in years of schooling is .2 years. In contrast, in the 40 to 54 age group, the average performance gap between White and Black adults is much larger, ranging from 65 to 75 points. The corresponding difference in average years of education is 1.6 years.

Across the age groups, there are even larger differences in average literacy proficiencies and years of schooling between White adults and respondents of Hispanic origin. Among 16- to 18-year-olds, the difference in average years of schooling between these two groups is 1.1 years, and the proficiency differences range from 47 to 53 points across the scales. Among 40- to 54-year-olds, on the other hand, the difference in average years of schooling is 3.2 years, and the proficiency gap is between 84 and 89 points on each scale.

For White adults and those of Asian/Pacific Islander origin, a different pattern is evident. The numbers of Asian/Pacific Islander adults in the 16 to 18, 55 to 64, and 65 and older age groups are too small to provide reliable proficiency estimates. In the age categories for which data are available, however, White adults outperformed Asian/Pacific Islander adults, but there are no significant differences between the two groups in average years of schooling. It is noteworthy that the performance gap between White and Asian/ Pacific Islander adults is relatively small in the 19 to 24 age group.

In making the comparisons between White adults and those of either Hispanic or Asian/Pacific Islander origin, it is important to remember that first language spoken and country of birth may contribute substantially to the proficiency differences that are observed.

Differences Between Adults in Various Racial/Ethnic Groups in Average Literacy Proficiencies and Average Years of Schooling, by Age

Differences Between White and Black Adults

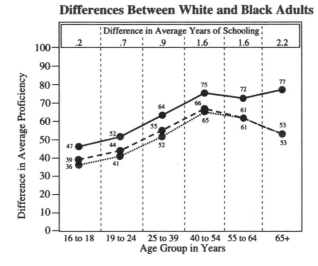

Differences Between White and Hispanic Adults

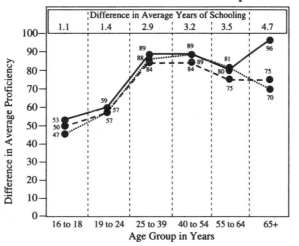

Differences Between White and Asian/Pacific Islander Adults*

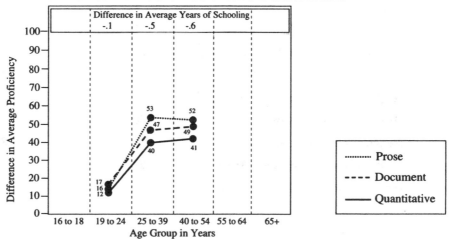

*The number of adults of Asian/Pacific Islander origin who were in the 16 to 18, 55 to 64, and 65 and older age groups were too small to provide reliable proficiency estimates.

Source: U.S. Department of Education, National Center for Education Statistics, National Adult Literacy Survey, 1992.

Country of Birth and Racial/Ethnic Differences

Many adults immigrate to the United States from places where English is not the national language. Not surprisingly, individuals born in this country tend to be more proficient in English than those born outside of this country, who are likely to have learned English as a second language. To better understand the differences in performance among various racial/ethnic groups, then, it is helpful to examine the proportion of each group that was born inside and outside the United States.

Nearly all White (96 percent) and Black (95 percent) adults and most respondents of Puerto Rican origin (80 percent) said they were born in the United States (TABLE 1.7). On the other hand, relatively small proportions of Asian/Pacific Islander (22 percent), Central/South American (21 percent), and Cuban (11 percent) adults were born in this country. About half of the Mexican adults and approximately 68 percent of the Hispanic/Other adults reported being born in the United States.

With one exception, individuals born in the United States tended to outperform their peers who were born abroad (FIGURE 1.9). The exception

NALS _____ Table 1.7

Percentages of Adults Born in the United States and in Other Countries or Territories, by Race/Ethnicity

Race/Ethnicity	Born in the United States	Born in Other Countries or Territories
White	96	4
Black	95	6
Asian or Pacific Islander	22	78
American Indian or Alaskan Native	100	0*
Other	24	76
Hispanic/Mexican	54	46
Hispanic/Puerto Rican	80	20
Hispanic/Cuban	11	89
Hispanic/Central or South American	21	79
Hispanic/Other	68	32

*Percentages below .5 are rounded to 0.

Source: U.S. Department of Education, National Center for Education Statistics, National Adult Literacy Survey, 1992.

Figure 1.9

Average Literacy Proficiencies, by Country of Birth and Race/Ethnicity

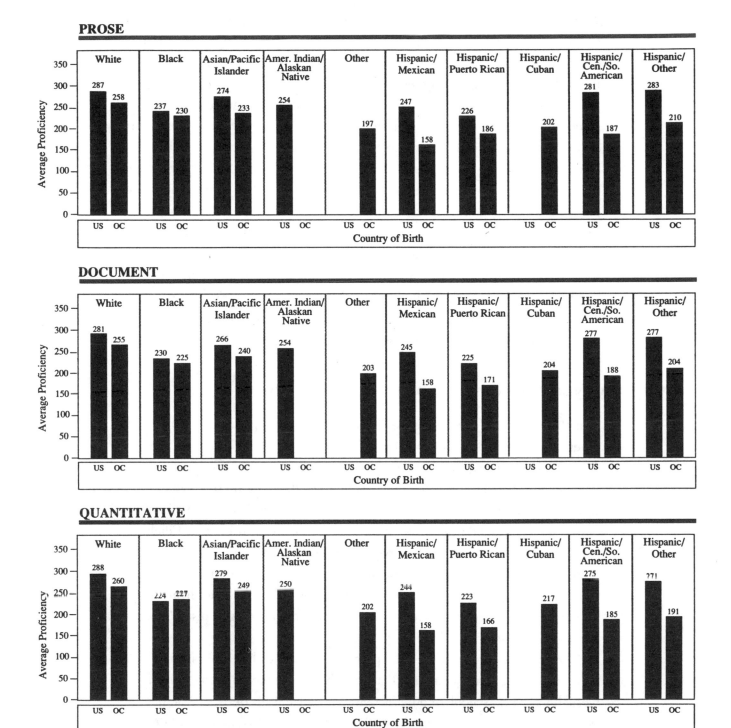

Note: The numbers of "Other" and Hispanic/Cuban adults who were born in the United States, and of American Indian/Alaskan Native adults who were born in other countries, are too small to provide reliable proficiency estimates.

US: United States   OC: Other Country or Territory

Source: U.S. Department of Education, National Center for Education Statistics, National Adult Literacy Survey, 1992.

appears among Black adults, where the differences in average performance range only from 3 to 7 points across the scales and are not significant. Across the three literacy scales, the average proficiencies of native-born Mexican, Puerto Rican, Central/South American, and Hispanic/Other adults are 40 to 94 points higher than those of their foreign-born peers. For White and Asian/Pacific Islander adults, the differences range from 26 to 41 points across the scales.

Indeed, when the differences in literacy proficiencies among various racial/ethnic groups are viewed through the lens of country of birth, the pattern of results that appears in Figure 1.6 changes substantially. When one takes country of birth into consideration, there are no significant differences between the prose and document proficiencies of native-born Central/South American or Hispanic/Other adults and the proficiencies of native-born White adults. Further, on all three scales, native-born Black and Puerto Rican individuals demonstrated about the same average proficiencies. The average scores of native-born Asian/Pacific Islander adults were similar to those of White adults, and to those of respondents who reported Central/South American and Hispanic/Other origins. Though some of the differences among these groups appear to be large, they did not reach statistical significance.

Results by Type of Illness, Disability, or Impairment

The National Adult Literacy Survey included a series of questions about illnesses and disabilities, making it possible to examine the literacy skills of adults with various types of conditions. One question asked respondents whether they had a physical, mental, or other health condition that kept them from participating fully in work, school, housework, or other activities. Two other questions asked whether they had visual or hearing difficulties. Finally, respondents were asked whether they had a learning disability, any mental or emotional condition, mental retardation, a speech disability, a physical disability, a long-term illness (for six months or more), or any other health impairment. Respondents were permitted to report each type of disability or condition they had.

Overall, 12 percent of the total population said they had a physical, mental, or other health condition that kept them from participating fully in work, housework, school, or other activities (TABLE 1.8). Between 6 and 9 percent reported vision or hearing difficulties, physical disabilities, long-term illnesses, or other health impairments, and about 3 percent reported having a learning disability. Very few individuals — 2 percent or less of the population — reported having some form of mental retardation, a mental or emotional condition, or a speech disability.

Percentages of Adults Who Reported Having a Physical, Mental, or Other Health Condition

Type of Condition	Total Population
Physical, mental, or other health condition	12
Visual difficulty	7
Hearing difficulty	7
Learning disability	3
Mental or emotional condition	2
Mental retardation	0*
Speech disability	1
Physical disability	9
Long-term illness	8
Other health impairment	6

*Percentages below .5 are rounded to 0.

Source: U.S. Department of Education, National Center for Education Statistics, National Adult Literacy Survey, 1992.

When the literacy levels and proficiencies of respondents who said they had an illness, disability, or impairment are compared with the literacy levels and proficiencies of adults in the total population, sharp contrasts are evident. Without exception, adults with any type of disability, difficulty, or illness were more likely than those in the total population to perform in the lowest literacy levels. Some conditions appear to have a stronger relationship with literacy than others, however (FIGURE 1.10).

Adults with mental retardation, for example, were about four times more likely than their peers in the total population to perform in Level 1 on the prose, document, and quantitative scales. On the prose scale, 87 percent of the respondents with mental retardation were in this level, compared with 21 percent of adults in the population as a whole.

Figure 1.10

Literacy Levels and Average Literacy Proficiencies, by Type of Physical, Mental, or Other Health Condition, Compared with the Total Population

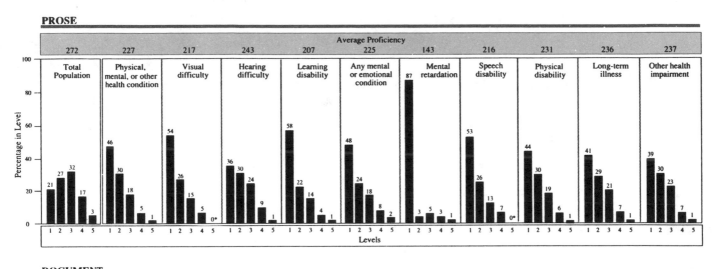

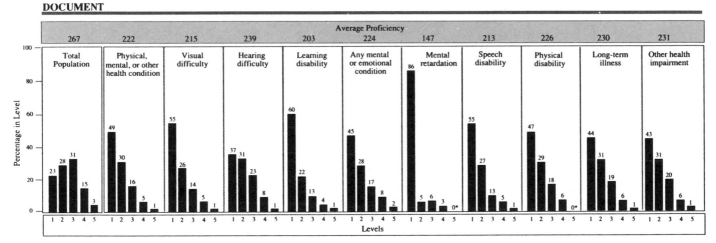

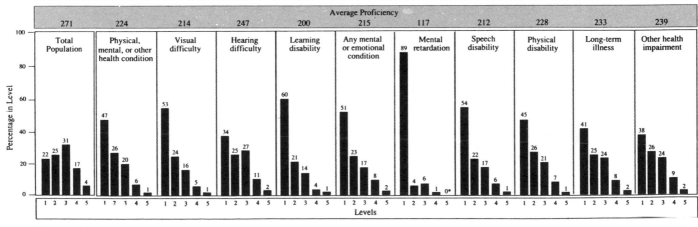

*Percentages below .5 are rounded to 0.

Level 1 (0 to 225)   **Level 2** (226 to 275)   **Level 3** (276 to 325)   **Level 4** (326 to 375)   **Level 5** (376 to 500)

Source: U.S. Department of Education, National Center for Education Statistics, National Adult Literacy Survey, 1992.

The performance gaps were smaller for the other disability groups, but they were still substantial. On each scale, more than half of the individuals with vision difficulties performed in Level 1 (53 to 55 percent), for example, and another 24 to 26 percent performed in Level 2. A similar pattern appears for those who reported having speech or learning disabilities; between 53 and 60 percent of the respondents with either of these disabilities had scores in the range for Level 1 on each scale, and 21 to 27 percent performed in Level 2.

These differences in the distributions of performance across the literacy levels are echoed in the average proficiency scores. Adults who reported having mental retardation demonstrated the weakest skills of all the groups examined. On the quantitative scale, for example, their average score was 117, which lies in the low end of Level 1. Respondents with learning disabilities had an average score of 200 on this scale, while the scores of those with a speech (212) or visual difficulty (214) or a mental or emotional condition (215) were slightly higher. The average quantitative proficiency of respondents who reported having a physical, mental, or health condition that impaired their ability to participate fully in activities was 224.

Groups whose average proficiency scores were in the low end of the Level 2 range on the quantitative scale included adults who said they had a physical disability (228) or a long-term illness (233). Individuals with hearing difficulties had higher average quantitative proficiencies (247), as well as higher prose and document proficiencies (243 and 239, respectively), than adults who reported other disabilities or conditions.

Finally, it is interesting to note the average performance differences between individuals who reported having certain disabilities and adults in the population as a whole. The smallest gap was between those who said they had difficulty hearing and adults in the population overall; the difference was 24 to 29 points on each literacy scale. Across the other groups, the performance gap between those who reported having a particular disability or illness and those in the total population ranged from 32 to 71 points. The only exception was among adults who reported having some form of mental retardation; here the gap ranged from 120 to 154 points across the scales.

Results by Region

Regional differences in average literacy proficiency are found on all three scales (FIGURE 1.11). Adults living in the Northeast and those living in the South performed similarly, on average. Further, the average proficiencies of adults in the Midwest and those in the West are comparable. However, adults in the Northeast and South demonstrated lower proficiencies, on average, than adults living in the Midwest and West regions of the country.

These differences may be attributable partly to regional variations in demographic characteristics such as country of birth or average years of schooling. These variables by themselves, however, do not provide a simple explanation for the proficiency differences across the regions (TABLE 1.9).

Comparing the data in Figure 1.11 and Table 1.9, it is apparent that adults residing in the West outperformed adults in the South and the Northeast regions, yet the West also had the highest percentage of individuals born outside the United States. Further, while adults living in the Midwest and the West outperformed those in the Northeast, the average number of years of schooling completed by adults in these regions was about the same. In contrast, adults in the West demonstrated higher average proficiencies than their peers in the South, and also reported significantly higher average years of schooling. It therefore appears that no single variable accounts for the regional variations in literacy proficiencies.

Results by Sex

The performance results for men and women differ across the three literacy scales (FIGURE 1.11). On the prose scale, the average proficiencies of women (273) and men (272) are about the same; the difference of 1 point is not significant. In contrast, men's average document (269) and quantitative proficiencies (277) are significantly higher than those of women (265 and 266). The sex differences on these scales are 4 and 11 points, respectively.

The fact that women tend to live longer than men and that literacy proficiencies tend to be lower for older adults, as seen earlier in this section, may contribute to the performance differences between the two sexes. So may other variables such as years of schooling, country of birth, and racial/ethnic background.

Literacy Levels and Average Literacy Proficiencies, by Region and Sex

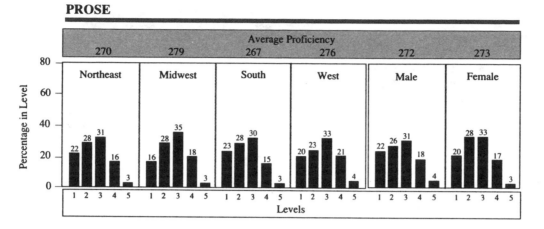

PROSE

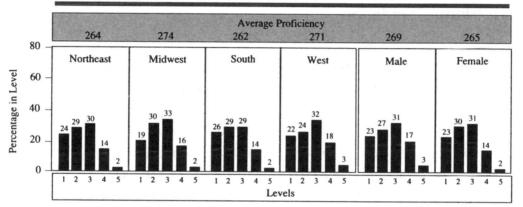

DOCUMENT

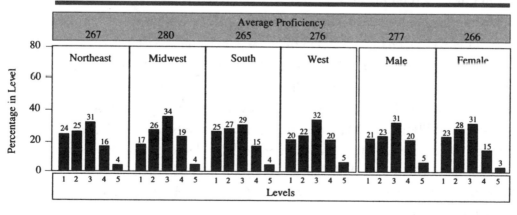

QUANTITATIVE

Level 1 (0 to 225)   **Level 2** (226 to 275)   **Level 3** (276 to 325)   **Level 4** (326 to 375)   **Level 5** (376 to 500)

Source: U.S. Department of Education, National Center for Education Statistics, National Adult Literacy Survey, 1992.

Percentages of Adults Born in Other Countries or Territories, and Average Years of Schooling, by Region

	Northeast	Midwest	South	West
Percentage of adults born in other countries or territories	14	3	7	18
Average years of schooling	12.5	12.5	12.2	12.6

Source: U.S. Department of Education, National Center for Education Statistics, National Adult Literacy Survey, 1992.

Results for the Prison Population

In addition to assessing individuals residing in households, the National Adult Literacy Survey evaluated a national sample of inmates in federal and state prisons. The survey included only those adults incarcerated in prisons both because more than half the nation's inmates are in these institutions and because prisons hold individuals for longer periods of time than do either jails or community-based facilities. Imprisoned adults make up a relatively small percentage of the total adult population in the United States, but their inclusion in this survey ensures better estimates of the literacy proficiencies of the adult population and allows for separate reporting of the literacy skills of adults in this important population.

The demographic characteristics of adults in prison were not representative of the characteristics of the total population (TABLE 1.10). The prison population tended to be both younger and less educated than adults in the nation as a whole, and most adults in prison were male. For example, males made up 48 percent of the total population but constituted 94 percent of those in prisons. In addition, only 20 percent of imprisoned adults reported having completed some postsecondary education or a college degree, while 42 percent of the adult population as a whole had gone beyond high school or a GED. Fully 80 percent of prisoners were below age 40, compared with 51 percent of the total population.

Percentages of Adults in Various Demographic Groups, Prison and Total Populations

	Prison Population	Total Population
Race/Ethnicity		
White	35	76
Black	44	11
Asian or Pacific Islander	1	2
American Indian or Alaskan Native	2	1
Other	1	0*
Hispanic groups	17	10
Sex		
Male	94	48
Female	6	52
Highest Level of Education Completed		
0 to 8 years	14	10
9 to 12 years	35	13
High school diploma	14	27
GED	17	4
Some college	16	21
College degree	4	21
Age		
16 to 18	2	5
19 to 24	21	13
25 to 39	57	33
40 to 54	17	23
55 to 64	2	10
65 and older	1	16

*Percentages below .5 are rounded to 0.

Source: U.S. Department of Education, National Center for Education Statistics, National Adult Literacy Survey, 1992.

Individuals in prison were also considerably different from the total population in terms of their racial/ethnic characteristics. Adults in prisons were considerably less likely to be White (35 percent) than adults in the total population (76 percent), and less likely to be Asian/Pacific Islander (1 percent, compared with 2 percent). In contrast, adults of Hispanic origin were overrepresented in the prison population. Seventeen percent of those in prison reported being of Hispanic origin, compared with 10 percent in the population as a whole. Similarly, Black and American Indian/Alaskan Native adults were overrepresented in the prison population. For example, Black adults made up 11 percent of the total population but accounted for about 44 percent of adults held in state and federal prisons.

Given the relationship between level of education and literacy and between race/ethnicity and literacy, it is not surprising that the prison population performed significantly worse (by 26 to 35 points) than the total population on each of the literacy scales (FIGURE 1.12).

In terms of the five literacy levels, the proportion of prisoners in Level 1 on each scale (31 to 40 percent) is larger than that of adults in the total population (21 to 23 percent). Conversely, the percentage of prisoners who demonstrated skills in Levels 4 and 5 (4 to 7 percent) is far smaller than the proportion of adults in the total population who performed in those levels (18 to 21 percent).

Summary

On each of the literacy scales, between 21 and 23 percent of the adults surveyed, representing some 40 to 44 million individuals nationwide, demonstrated proficiencies in the range for Level 1. Though all adults in this level displayed limited skills, their characteristics were quite diverse. Some of these adults succeeded in performing the less challenging assessment tasks, while others had such limited skills that they were able to respond to only a part of the survey. Many of the individuals in this level were born in other countries; had not attended school beyond the eighth grade; were elderly; or had a disability, illness, or impairment.

Across the literacy scales, some 25 and 28 percent of the adults surveyed, representing another 48 to 54 million adults nationwide, demonstrated performance in Level 2. Nearly one-third, representing some 60 million adults, performed in Level 3, and another 15 to 17 percent — or approximately 30 million — were in Level 4. Only 3 to 4 percent of the respondents performed in the highest level of prose, document, or quantitative literacy. In population terms, this represents only 6 to 8 million adults nationwide.

The survey results reveal an interesting contrast between individuals' demonstrated English literacy skills and their perceptions of their level of proficiency. Of the adults who performed in the lowest level on each scale, the vast majority said they were able to read or write English well. Similarly, although individuals in the lowest literacy level were more likely than those in the higher levels to say that they get a lot of help from family members and friends in performing everyday literacy tasks, the proportions who said they get such help were lower than might be expected.

Literacy Levels and Average Literacy Proficiencies for the Prison and Total Populations

PROSE

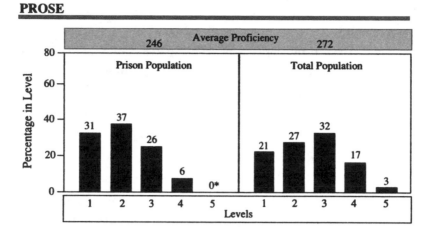

DOCUMENT

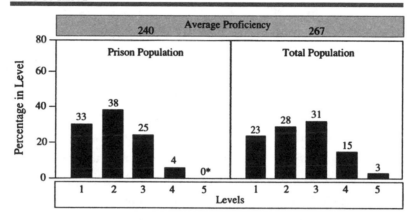

QUANTITATIVE

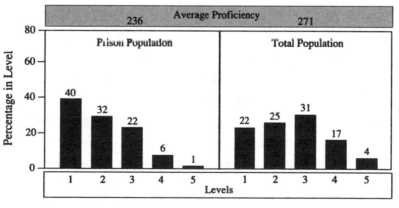

*Percentages below .5 are rounded to 0.

Level 1 (0 to 225)   Level 2 (226 to 275)   Level 3 (276 to 325)   Level 4 (326 to 375)   Level 5 (376 to 500)

Source: U.S. Department of Education, National Center for Education Statistics, National Adult Literacy Survey, 1992.

A strong relationship exists between education and literacy. Adults who had completed high school demonstrated significantly higher average prose, document, and quantitative proficiencies than those who had not, and individuals whose highest level of education was a college degree performed far better, on average, than those with high school diplomas or lower levels of education. The survey results also reveal a strong association between adults' literacy proficiencies and their parents' educational attainments, although the impact of one's own education appears to be greater.

An analysis of the performance of adults in different age groups indicates that prose and quantitative literacy skills increase from the teenage years up to the middle forties, then decline sharply across the older age groups. On the document scale, the rise in proficiency scores across the younger age groups is more gradual, but still there are marked declines across the two older age groups. One variable that helps to explain the proficiency decline across the age groups is education; older adults tended to have completed fewer years of schooling than adults in all but the youngest age group.

Differences in performance are also evident across the various racial and ethnic populations studied. The average prose, document, and quantitative proficiencies of White adults, for example, were significantly higher than those of adults in all the other racial/ethnic groups examined. These differences in performance can be explained in part by differences in average years of schooling and by respondents' country of birth.

Respondents who reported having any type of physical, mental, or health condition demonstrated much more limited literacy skills than those in the population as a whole. Some conditions — such as mental retardation, learning disabilities, or vision problems — appear to have a stronger relationship with literacy than other conditions.

Adults residing in the Northeast and South demonstrated lower average skills than adults living in the Midwest and West. Further, while the average prose literacy scores of men and women were nearly identical, men outperformed women in document and quantitative literacy.

Finally, incarcerated individuals were far more likely than adults in the total population to be in the lower levels on the prose, document, and quantitative scales. The relatively weak performance of the prison population can be attributed at least in part to the demographic characteristics of incarcerated individuals, which differ substantially from the characteristics of the adult population as a whole.

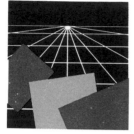

SECTION II

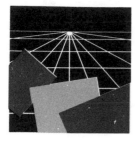

SECTION II

The Connection Between Adults' Literacy Skills and Their Social and Economic Characteristics

The first section of this report provided a portrait of literacy in the United States, describing the literacy levels and proficiencies of the adult population and of many different subpopulations. In this section, the focus shifts to the connections between literacy and particular aspects of adults' lives.

Previous studies have identified certain practices and conditions that are related to literacy.[1] Accordingly, adults participating in this survey were asked to report on their voting experience, reading practices, economic status, recent employment, and occupations. Their responses make it possible to examine how various aspects of adults' lives vary according to their literacy proficiencies — that is, to see what connections exist between literacy and an array of social and economic variables. Are those in the higher literacy levels more likely to get information from print than those in the lower levels? Are they more likely to be employed, hold certain kinds of jobs, or earn better wages? These types of questions are addressed in the pages that follow.

Literacy and Voting

One question in the survey asked respondents to indicate whether or not they had voted in a state or national election in the United States in the past five years. A clear relationship was found between literacy skills and voting practices. On all three scales, there was a significant increase across the literacy levels in the percentages of adults who reported voting in a recent state or national election (FIGURE 2.1). On the prose scale, for example, 89 percent of the individuals in Level 5 who were eligible to vote said they had voted in the past five years, compared with just over half (55 percent) of the individuals in Level 1.

---

[1] G. Berlin and A. Sum. (1988). *Toward a More Perfect Union*. New York, NY: Ford Foundation. Statistics Canada. (1991). *Adult Literacy in Canada: Results of a National Study.* Ottawa, Canada: Statistics Canada. I.S. Kirsch and A. Jungeblut. (1992, September). *Profiling the Literacy Proficiencies of JTPA and ES/UI Populations: Final Report to the Department of Labor.* Princeton, NJ: Educational Testing Service.

Percentages of Adults Who Voted in a National or State Election in the Past Five Years, by Literacy Level

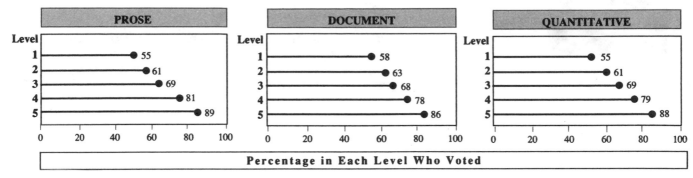

Note: This figure represents the percentages of adults who voted, of those who were eligible to vote.

Level 1	0 to 225
Level 2	226 to 275
Level 3	276 to 325
Level 4	326 to 375
Level 5	376 to 500

Source: U.S. Department of Education, National Center for Education Statistics, National Adult Literacy Survey, 1992.

Literacy and Reading Practices

Many different types of newspapers are published in this country, ranging from long, comprehensive daily newspapers to shorter and more informal community newspapers, which tend to be published on a weekly or biweekly basis. Together these print media keep readers informed about current events in their communities, the nation, and the world.

Because the newspaper plays such an important role in disseminating information in this society, the National Adult Literacy Survey asked participants to indicate how often they read the newspaper and to identify the parts of the newspaper that they generally read. Respondents were also asked to report to what extent they relied on newspapers or magazines, radio or television, and family or friends for information about current events, public affairs, and government.

The responses indicate that newspaper reading was very common among readers in all levels of literacy, although adults in the lower levels were less likely than those in the higher levels to report that they read the newspaper every day and were more likely to say that they never read it. Finally, while virtually all adults — regardless of their literacy levels — reported getting some or a lot of information about current events from television or radio, those in the higher literacy levels were more likely than those in the lower levels to say they also get some or a lot of information from print media.

Frequency of Newspaper Reading

On all three literacy scales, adults in the lowest level were less likely than those in the higher levels to report reading the newspaper every day; 35 to 40 percent of those in Level 1, approximately half of the adults in Levels 2 and 3, and between half and two-thirds of those in Levels 4 and 5 said they read the paper this often (FIGURE 2.2). Likewise, respondents who performed in the lowest level (19 to 21 percent across the scales) were much more likely than those in the highest level (1 percent) to say they never read the newspaper.

NALS   **Figure 2.2**

Percentages of Adults Who Read the Newspaper, by Literacy Level

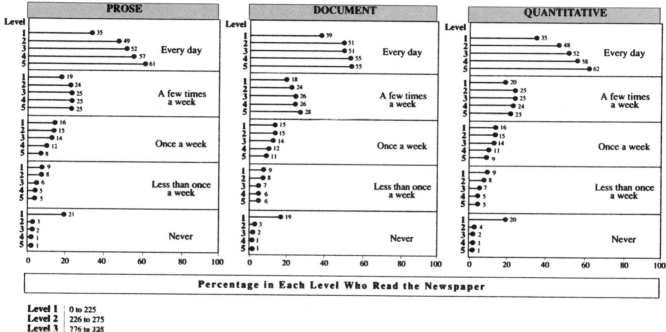

Percentage in Each Level Who Read the Newspaper

Level 1	0 to 225
Level 2	226 to 275
Level 3	276 to 325
Level 4	326 to 375
Level 5	376 to 500

Source: U.S. Department of Education, National Center for Education Statistics, National Adult Literacy Survey, 1992.

Aspects of Newspaper Reading

Participants were asked to indicate which parts of the newspaper they generally read, and their answers were combined with the responses to the previous question to determine what percentages of those who read the newspaper at least once a week read certain parts. The ten categories listed in the survey questionnaire, each of which reflects somewhat different literacy demands, were grouped into five categories for reporting purposes: the news, editorial, and financial pages; sports; home, fashion, health, and reviews of books, movies, and art; TV, movie, and concert listings, as well as classified ads and other advertisements; and comics, horoscopes, and advice columns.

Among adults who read the newspaper at least once a week, the vast majority — even of those who performed in Level 1 on each scale — said they generally read the news, editorial, or financial sections (FIGURE 2.3). Virtually all adults in the higher levels said they read these sections of the newspaper at least once a week.

Though many of the differences are small, there are variations across the literacy levels in the percentages of adults who reported reading other parts of the newspaper. For example, about 45 percent of the newspaper readers who performed in Level 1 on the quantitative scale said they generally look at the sports pages, compared with 58 percent of those in Level 5. Some 74 percent of the newspaper readers in Level 1 on the prose scale reported reading the home, fashion, health, or reviews sections, compared with 86 percent in Level 5. Across the levels on each scale, 76 to 88 percent said they read the classifieds and listings, and 66 to 73 percent reported reading the comics, horoscopes, or advice columns.

Another perspective on the relationship between literacy and reading practices can be gained by comparing the average proficiencies of respondents who read certain sections of the newspaper and those who do not (TABLE 2.1). On each of the literacy scales, newspaper readers who generally skip the news, editorials, or financial sections had average proficiency scores of 248 on the prose and document scales and 250 on the quantitative scale. These scores are significantly lower (by 28 to 34 points) than the scores of those who said they read these sections on a regular basis. When one reexamines the responses shown in Figure 2.3, the reason for these differences is clear. The relatively few adults (1 to 8 percent) who said they tend to skip these sections were much more likely to be in the lowest levels. As a result, on each scale, they demonstrated considerably lower average scores than the vast majority of newspaper readers who said they generally do read these sections.

Sports reporting in newspapers often includes tables, lists, and quantitative measures of performance. There are significant differences in

Among Adults Who Read the Newspaper at Least Once a Week, Percentages Who Read Certain Parts, by Literacy Level

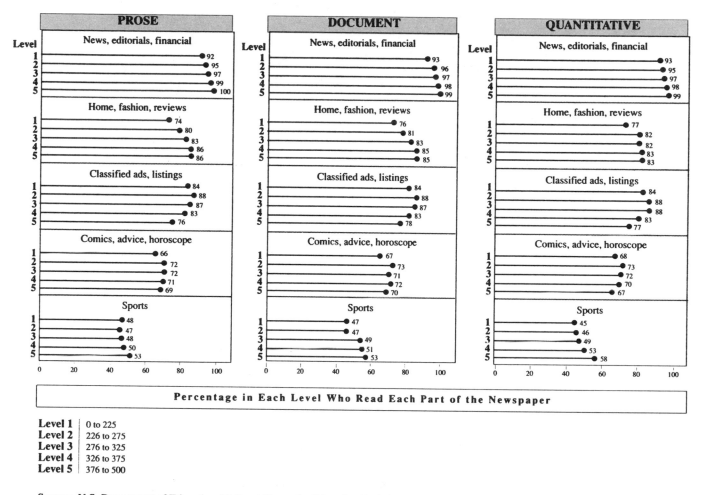

Percentage in Each Level Who Read Each Part of the Newspaper

Level 1	0 to 225
Level 2	226 to 275
Level 3	276 to 325
Level 4	326 to 375
Level 5	376 to 500

Source: U.S. Department of Education, National Center for Education Statistics, National Adult Literacy Survey, 1992.

average document and quantitative performance between those who choose to read the sports pages and those who do not. While on the quantitative scale the proficiency gap is 8 points, on the document scale it is only 3 points. On the prose scale, the 2-point difference between sports page readers and nonreaders is not statistically significant. Once again, these results can be better understood by reexamining the differences across the literacy levels in the percentages of newspaper readers who reported choosing the sports pages, particularly for the quantitative scale. In this dimension of literacy, readers in the lowest level (45 percent) were considerably less likely than those in the highest level (58 percent) to say they generally read this section. On the other hand, there were relatively small differences (of 5 to 6 points) across the prose

Table 2.1

Among Adults Who Read the Newspaper at Least Once a Week, Average Literacy Proficiencies, by Newspaper Reading Practices

	Average Prose Proficiency		Average Document Proficiency		Average Quantitative Proficiency	
	Yes	No	Yes	No	Yes	No
News, editorials, financial	282	248	276	248	281	250
Home, fashion, reviews	284	267	277	264	282	271
Classified ads, listings	280	282	274	274	280	282
Comics, advice, horoscope	282	277	276	271	280	279
Sports	282	280	276	273	284	276

Source: U.S. Department of Education, National Center for Education Statistics, National Adult Literacy Survey, 1992.

and document literacy levels in the percentages of adults who said they generally read this section.

The home, fashion, health, and reviews sections typically consist of connected prose with some illustrations and tables. Newspaper readers who performed in the higher levels on each scale were more likely to report that they read these sections, while those in the lowest level were more likely to report skipping them. The differences were greatest on the prose scale, and this is reflected in the average proficiency results: The average prose scores of newspaper readers who generally read these sections were considerably higher (284 compared with 267) than those of readers who said they tend to skip them.

Different patterns are evident for the other aspects of newspaper reading. On each scale, the percentages of newspaper readers who said they generally look at the classified ads and listings varied across the literacy levels, rising from 84 percent of those in Level 1 to 88 percent in Level 2 before declining to some three-quarters of the respondents in Level 5. Yet there are no significant differences in average prose, document, or quantitative proficiency between newspaper readers who said they generally read these sections and those who do not. In contrast, newspaper readers who reported that they generally read the comics, horoscopes, or advice columns demonstrated average prose and document proficiencies that were slightly (5 points) higher than those of individuals who said they do not generally read these sections. As shown in Figure 2.3, though, the percentages of adults who reported reading these parts of the newspaper varied little across the levels on each literacy scale.

Reliance on Print and Nonprint Sources of Information

Survey participants were asked to indicate the sources from which they get information about current events, public affairs, and government. Their responses indicate that while many adults get their information from family members and friends, the overwhelming majority get either some or a lot of news from nonprint media — between 93 and 97 percent reported using radio or television to obtain information about current events, public affairs and government. (FIGURE 2.4).

NALS   **Figure 2.4**

Percentages of Adults Who Get Information About Current Events from Various Sources, by Literacy Level

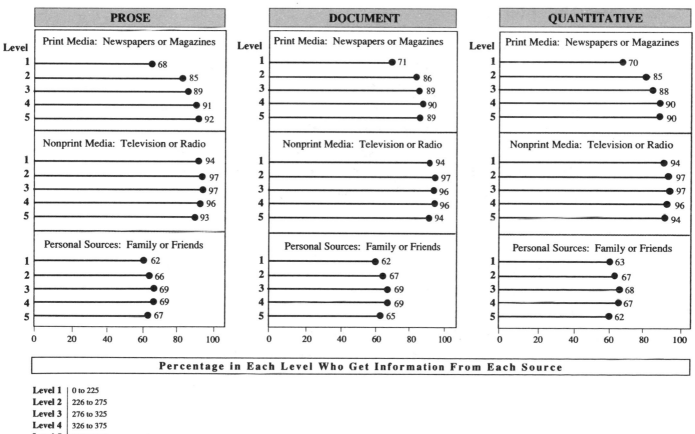

Percentage in Each Level Who Get Information From Each Source

Level 1	0 to 225
Level 2	226 to 275
Level 3	276 to 325
Level 4	326 to 375
Level 5	376 to 500

Source: U.S. Department of Education, National Center for Education Statistics, National Adult Literacy Survey, 1992.

Individuals in the lower literacy levels were less likely to use print media as an information source than were adults in the higher levels. Across the scales, only 68 to 71 percent of the respondents in Level 1 said they get information from newspapers or magazines. Adults performing in the higher literacy levels, on the other hand, were more likely to get information from print media: 88 to 92 percent of those in Levels 3, 4, and 5 on the scales said they obtain information from newspapers or magazines.

While one might expect adults in the lower literacy levels to rely more heavily on friends or family for information, this hypothesis was not supported by the results. Across the levels, there are small but significant differences in the percentages of adults who said they get some or a lot of information from personal sources. For example, on the prose scale, larger percentages of adults in Levels 3 and 4 than in Levels 1 and 2 reported getting some or a lot of information on current events from friends or family. On the document and quantitative scales, the percentages of adults who reported getting information from personal sources increased from Level 1 to Level 3, then declined significantly between Levels 4 and 5.

Literacy and Economic Status

To explore the connection between literacy and economic status, the National Adult Literacy Survey gathered information on respondents' income. Some of the questions requested data on wages, while others asked for information on sources of income. When the responses to these questions are examined by literacy level, strong relationships between literacy and economic status are evident. Adults in the lower literacy levels were far more likely than those in the higher levels to be in poverty and were far more likely to be on food stamps than to report receiving interest from savings.

Poverty Status

Adults who participated in the NALS were asked to indicate their personal and household income. These self-reported data were then used to divide adults into two categories — poor or near poor, and not poor — using federal poverty guidelines. Across the three scales, 41 to 44 percent of those in Level 1 were in poverty, compared with only 4 to 6 percent of the adults in the highest level (FIGURE 2.5). These results underscore literacy's strong connection to economic status.

Percentages of Adults in Poverty, by Literacy Level

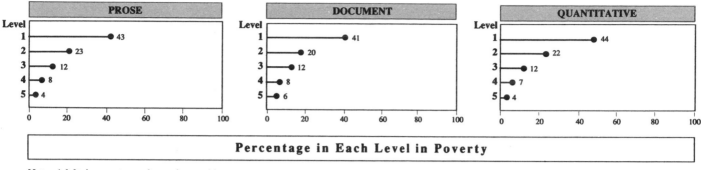

Note: Adults in poverty are those who are either poor or near poor.

Level 1	0 to 225
Level 2	226 to 275
Level 3	276 to 325
Level 4	326 to 375
Level 5	376 to 500

Source: U.S. Department of Education, National Center for Education Statistics, National Adult Literacy Survey, 1992.

Sources of Nonwage Income and Support

Survey participants provided detailed information on the types of nonwage income and support they or anyone in their family had received in the year preceding the survey. Two particular types of nonwage income which reflect socioeconomic status are contrasted here. The skills of those who received food stamps are of interest, because this program is publicly funded. Further, the competencies of adults who received interest from savings or other bank accounts are of interest, because savings help to provide a buffer in the event of interruptions in earnings.

Adults who performed in Level 1 on the prose scale were far more likely than those who performed in Level 5 to report that their family received food stamps (FIGURE 2.6). Only 1 percent of those in the highest prose level received food stamps, compared with 17 percent in the lowest level. Similar patterns are seen on the document and quantitative scales.

Conversely, the percentages of adults who reported receiving interest from savings in the past year increases significantly across the five levels on each scale. For example, 85 percent of adults in Level 5 on the quantitative scale earned interest from savings, compared with only 53 percent of those in Level 3 and just 23 percent of those in Level 1.

Percentages of Adults Who Received Certain Types of Nonwage Income or Support in the Past 12 Months, by Literacy Level

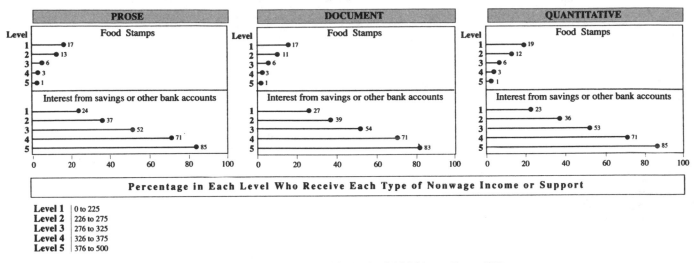

Level 1	0 to 225
Level 2	226 to 275
Level 3	276 to 325
Level 4	326 to 375
Level 5	376 to 500

Source: U.S. Department of Education, National Center for Education Statistics, National Adult Literacy Survey, 1992.

Literacy and Employment, Earnings, and Occupations

While our nation's concern over literacy skills appropriately encompasses all areas of life, much attention in recent years has been focused on the role literacy plays in the workplace. Recent reports have called into question the adequacy of America's current education and training system to fulfill its expected role in ensuring individual opportunity, increasing productivity, and strengthening America's competitiveness in a global economy.

The NALS background questionnaire asked respondents to report on their employment status, their weekly earnings, the number of weeks they worked in the previous year, and the type of job they held, if they worked. On average, individuals in the higher levels of literacy were more likely to be employed, earn higher wages, work more weeks per year, and be in professional, technical, or managerial occupations than respondents who displayed lower levels of skill.

Employment Status

Respondents were asked to indicate what their employment situation had been during the week before the survey. When their responses are compared with the performance results, it is clear that individuals with more limited literacy skills are less likely to be employed than those who demonstrated more advanced skills. On each of the literacy scales, more than half of the adults who demonstrated proficiencies in Level 1 were out of the labor force — that is, not employed and not looking for work — compared with only 10 to 18 percent of the adults performing in each of the two highest levels (FIGURE 2.7). On the other hand, some 30 percent of the individuals in Level 1 and nearly 45 percent of those in Level 2 had full-time employment, compared with about 64 to 75 percent of the respondents who performed in the two highest literacy levels.

The average proficiency results offer another perspective on the connection between literacy and labor force status. As seen in Figure 2.7, adults in the highest literacy levels were far more likely than those in the lowest levels to report being employed full time. As a result, the average proficiencies of full-time employees are quite high — 288, 284, and 290, across the three literacy scales (TABLE 2.2).

NALS _____ **Figure 2.7**

Percentages of Adults In and Out of the Labor Force, by Literacy Level

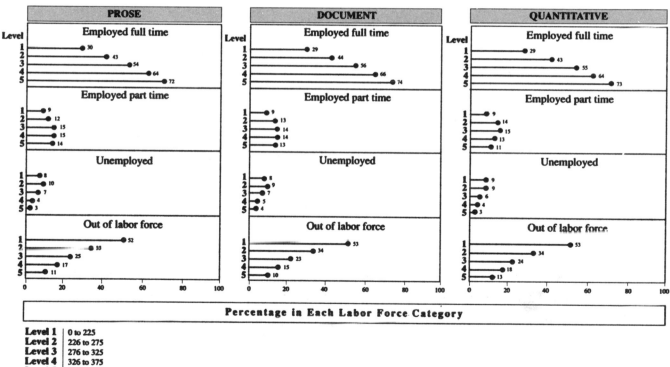

Level 1	0 to 225
Level 2	226 to 275
Level 3	276 to 325
Level 4	326 to 375
Level 5	376 to 500

Source: U.S. Department of Education, National Center for Education Statistics, National Adult Literacy Survey, 1992.

Average Literacy Proficiencies, by Labor Force Status

	Prose	Document	Quantitative
Employed full time	288	284	290
Employed part time	284	277	280
Unemployed	260	257	256
Out of labor force	246	237	241

Source: U.S. Department of Education, National Center for Education Statistics, National Adult Literacy Survey, 1992.

Working part time was more prevalent among adults in the higher literacy levels, though the differences across the levels were small. Accordingly, the average prose, document, and quantitative scores of part-time workers are only 4 to 10 points below those of adults working full time. Unemployment, on the other hand, was more prevalent among individuals who performed in the lowest literacy levels, and as a result, the average literacy proficiencies of unemployed adults are 27 to 34 points lower than those of full-time employees.

The average proficiencies of adults who were out of the labor force — 246, 237, and 241, across the three scales — were 42 to 49 points lower than those of individuals who were employed full time. These disparities can be attributed to the relatively high percentages of adults in the lower literacy levels who were out of the labor force.

Weeks Worked

All individuals who participated in the survey, regardless of their current or recent employment status, were asked how many weeks they had worked in the past 12 months. On each scale, individuals scoring in Levels 3, 4, and 5 worked more weeks in the past year than those performing in Level 2, who, in turn, worked more weeks than those in Level 1 (FIGURE 2.8).

Average Number of Weeks Worked in the Past 12 Months, by Literacy Level

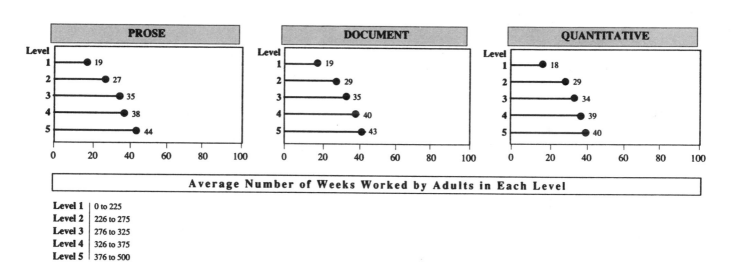

Level 1	0 to 225
Level 2	226 to 275
Level 3	276 to 325
Level 4	326 to 375
Level 5	376 to 500

Source: U.S. Department of Education, National Center for Education Statistics, National Adult Literacy Survey, 1992.

Clearly, the number of weeks worked increases dramatically across the literacy levels. While respondents who demonstrated proficiency in the lowest level on each scale worked, on average, only about 19 weeks a year, individuals in the three highest levels reported working about twice as many weeks — between 34 and 44.

Earnings

Individuals who were either working full time or part time or were on leave from their jobs the week before the survey were asked to report their weekly wage or salary before deductions. Given that individuals who performed in the higher levels were more likely than those in the lower levels to be in the work force and to have worked more weeks in the past year, it is not surprising that these individuals reported earning significantly more money each week (FIGURE 2.9).

On each literacy scale, the median earnings of individuals performing in Level 1 were approximately $230 to 240 each week. In comparison, those who performed in Level 3 reported earning $340 to $350 (or about $110 more), while those in Level 4 reported earning $462 to $472 (or nearly $250 more). For those who attained Level 5, the financial rewards were even greater. Individuals performing in this level on the quantitative scale, for example, had median earnings of $681 each week — roughly $450 more than individuals performing in Level 1 on that scale.

Figure 2.9

Median Weekly Wages, by Literacy Level

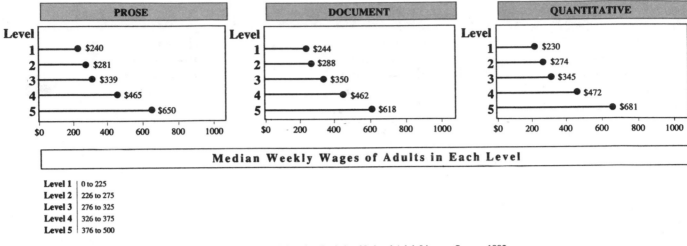

Level 1	0 to 225
Level 2	226 to 275
Level 3	276 to 325
Level 4	326 to 375
Level 5	376 to 500

Source: U.S. Department of Education, National Center for Education Statistics, National Adult Literacy Survey, 1992.

Occupations

While it would be useful to know the level of literacy skills required to find, hold, and succeed in various types of jobs, research is limited in this area. Some perspective on this question can be gained, however, by looking at the percentages of people within certain occupational categories who demonstrated various levels of literacy. Survey participants were asked to describe the type of work they performed in their current or most recent job, and this information was sorted into occupational categories using the Census Classification for Industries and Occupations. These categories were then recombined into four occupational groupings, and the percentages of respondents who worked in these categories of jobs were calculated. Twenty-four percent of the adults surveyed worked in managerial, professional, or technical jobs; 28 percent were in sales or clerical occupations; 29 percent worked in craft or service occupations; and 19 percent were in laborer, assembler, fishing, or farming jobs.

In all but the group of adults holding sales or clerical positions, the data show a strong relationship between the type of job that individuals held and their demonstrated level of literacy proficiency (FIGURE 2.10). This figure displays the percentages of adults in each literacy level who reported holding a particular type of job.

On all three literacy scales, individuals who performed in the highest levels were much more likely to report holding managerial, professional, or technical jobs than were respondents who performed in the lowest levels.

Percentages of Adults in Certain Occupational Categories, by Literacy Level

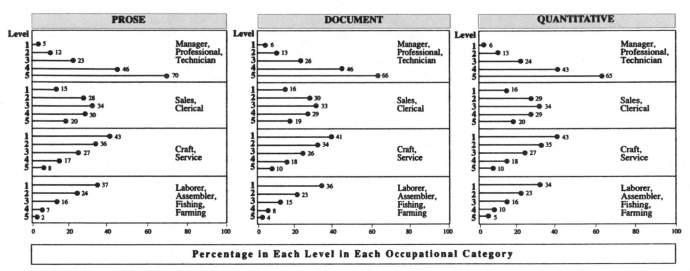

Percentage in Each Level in Each Occupational Category

Note: Overall, 24 percent of the adults surveyed reported holding managerial, professional, or technical jobs; 28 percent reported holding sales or clerical jobs; 29 percent reported holding craft or service jobs; and 19 percent reported holding laborer, assembler, fishing or farming jobs.

Level 1	0 to 225
Level 2	226 to 275
Level 3	276 to 325
Level 4	326 to 375
Level 5	376 to 500

Source: U.S. Department of Education, National Center for Education Statistics, National Adult Literacy Survey, 1992.

From 65 to 70 percent of those in Level 5 held these positions, compared with approximately 13 percent of the respondents performing in Level 2, and 6 percent of those performing in Level 1. Thus, the likelihood of being in a managerial, professional, or technical position declines sharply from Level 5 to Level 1. It is interesting to note, however, that small percentages of individuals in Levels 1 and 2 reported being in managerial, professional, or technical positions. While these data do not reveal what specific types of positions these individuals held, or how successful they were in negotiating the demands of these positions, it does appear that at least some individuals with limited skills are able to obtain managerial and professional jobs.

In contrast with these data, a far different pattern is evident among those holding craft or service jobs: On each scale, adults whose proficiency was in the Level 1 range were far more likely than individuals who performed in the Level 5 range to hold these types of jobs. On the quantitative scale, for example, 10 percent of those performing in Level 5 reported being in craft or service jobs, compared with approximately 18 percent in Level 4, 27 percent of those in Level 3, 35 percent in Level 2, and 43 percent of those in Level 1. A similar pattern is shown for those adults reporting laborer, assembler, fishing, or farming occupations.

356-371 0 - 93 - 4 : QL 3

The greatest variability in literacy proficiencies seems to occur among adults reporting sales or clerical jobs. The percentages of adults in these positions increase between Levels 1 and 2 and again between Levels 2 and 3, then decrease across the two highest levels.

These data show a strong relationship between one's literacy skills and one's occupation. It should be noted, however, that this relationship is likely to be quite complex. While adults with better literacy skills almost certainly have greater opportunities to obtain professional, managerial, or technical positions, it is also likely that many of these positions enable individuals to strengthen their literacy skills.

Summary

Individuals who participated in the National Adult Literacy Survey were asked to provide information on various aspects of their lives that have been found in previous research to be related to literacy. This self-reported information was used to explore the connections between literacy and various social and economic outcomes.

Newspaper reading appears to be very common among American adults, regardless of their demonstrated literacy skills. However, those who performed in the lowest literacy level were far more likely than those in the higher levels to say they never read a newspaper. Similarly, the vast majority of adults reported getting some or a lot of information about current events from television or radio, but those in the lower literacy levels were less likely than those in the higher levels to say they also get some or a lot of information from print media. In addition to these differences in reading practices by literacy level, the survey results reveal that adults with limited literacy proficiencies were far less likely to have voted in a recent state or national election than were those with more advanced competencies.

Strong relationships between literacy and economic status are also evident in the survey findings. Relatively high proportions of adults in the lower literacy levels were in poverty and received food stamps. On the other hand, relatively few reported receiving interest from savings, which helps to protect individuals from interruptions in earnings.

Further, individuals who performed in the lower levels of literacy proficiency were more likely than their more proficient counterparts to be unemployed or out of the labor force. They also tended to earn lower wages and work fewer weeks per year, and were more likely to be in craft, service, laborer, or assembler occupations than respondents who demonstrated higher levels of literacy performance.

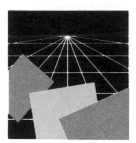

SECTION III

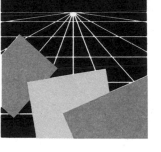

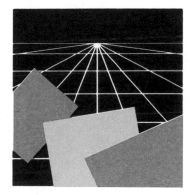

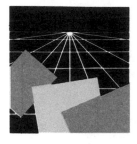

SECTION III

Interpreting the Literacy Scales

Building on the two earlier literacy surveys conducted by Educational Testing Service (ETS), the performance results from the National Adult Literacy Survey are reported on three literacy scales — prose, document, and quantitative — rather than on a single conglomerate scale. Each of the three literacy scales ranges from 0 to 500.

The purpose of this section of the report is to give meaning to the literacy scales — or, more specifically, to interpret the numerical scores that are used to represent adults' proficiencies on these scales. Toward this end, the section begins with a brief summary of the task development process and of the way in which the literacy levels are defined. A detailed description of the prose, document, and quantitative scales is then provided. The five levels on each scale are defined, and the skills and strategies needed to successfully perform the tasks in each level are discussed. Sample tasks are presented to illustrate the types of materials and task demands that characterize the levels on each scale. The section ends with a brief summary of the probabilities of successful performance on tasks within each level for individuals who demonstrated different proficiencies.

Building the Literacy Tasks

The literacy scales make it possible not only to summarize the literacy proficiencies of the total population and of various subpopulations, but also to determine the relative difficulty of the literacy tasks administered in the survey. That is, just as an individual receives a score according to his or her performance on the assessment tasks, each task receives a value according to its difficulty as determined by the performance of the adults who participated in the survey. Previous research conducted at ETS has shown that the difficulty of a literacy task, and therefore its placement on a particular literacy scale, is determined by three factors: the structure or linguistic format of the material, the content and/or the context from which it is selected, and the nature of the task, or what the individual is asked to do with the material.

Materials. The materials selected for inclusion in NALS reflect a variety of linguistic formats that adults encounter in their daily activities. Most of the prose materials used in the survey are expository — that is, they describe, define, or inform — since most of the prose that adults read is expository in nature; however, narratives and poetry are included, as well. The prose materials include an array of linguistic structures, ranging from texts that are highly organized both topically and visually to those that are loosely organized. They also include texts of varying lengths, from multiple-page magazine selections to short newspaper articles. All prose materials included in the survey were reproduced in their original format.

The document materials represent a wide variety of structures, which are characterized as tables, charts and graphs, forms, and maps, among other categories. Tables include matrix documents in which information is arrayed in rows and columns — for example, bus or airplane schedules, lists, or tables of numbers. Documents categorized as charts and graphs include pie charts, bar graphs, and line graphs. Forms are documents that require information to be filled in, while other structures include such materials as advertisements and coupons.

The quantitative tasks require the reader to perform arithmetic operations using numbers that are embedded in print. Since there are no materials that are unique to quantitative tasks, these tasks were based on prose materials and documents. Most quantitative tasks were, in fact, based on document structures.

Content and/or Contexts. Adults do not read printed or written materials in a vacuum. Rather, they read within a particular context or for a particular purpose. Accordingly, the NALS materials represent a variety of contexts and contents. Six such areas were identified: home and family; health and safety; community and citizenship; consumer economics; work; and leisure and recreation.

In selecting materials to represent these areas, efforts were made to include as broad a range as possible, as well as to select universally relevant contexts and contents. This was to ensure that the materials would not be so specialized as to be familiar only to certain groups. In this way, disadvantages for individuals with limited background knowledge were minimized.

Types of Tasks. After the materials were selected, tasks were developed to accompany the materials. These tasks were designed to simulate the ways in which people use various types of materials and to require different strategies for successful task completion. For both the prose and document scales, the tasks can be organized into three major categories: *locating, integrating,* and *generating* information. In the locating tasks, readers are asked to match information that is given in a question or directive with either literal or synonymous information in the text or document. Integrating tasks require the reader to incorporate two or more pieces of information located in different parts of the text or document. Generating tasks require readers not only to process information located in different parts of the material, but also to go beyond that information by drawing on their knowledge about a subject or by making broad text-based inferences.

Quantitative tasks require readers to perform arithmetic operations — addition, subtraction, multiplication, or division — either singly or in combination. In some tasks, the type of operation that must be performed is obvious from the wording of the question, while in other tasks the readers must infer which operation is to be performed. Similarly, the numbers that are required to perform the operation can, in some cases, be easily identified, while in others, the numbers that are needed are embedded in text. Moreover, some quantitative tasks require the reader to explain how the problem would be solved rather than perform the calculation, and on some tasks the use of a simple four-function calculator is required.

Defining the Literacy Levels

The relative difficulty of the assessment tasks reflects the interactions among the various task characteristics described here. As shown in Figure 1 in the Introduction to this report, the score point assigned to each task is the point at which the individuals with that proficiency score have a high probability of responding correctly. In this survey, an 80 percent probability of correct response was the criterion used. While some tasks were at the very low end of the scale and some at the very high end, most had difficulty values in the 200 to 400 range.

By assigning scale values to both the individuals and tasks, it is possible to see how well adults with varying proficiencies performed on tasks of varying difficulty. While individuals with low proficiency tend to perform well on tasks with difficulty values equivalent to or below their level of proficiency, they are less likely to succeed on tasks with higher difficulty values. This does not mean that individuals with low proficiency can never succeed on more difficult literacy tasks — that is, on tasks whose difficulty values are higher than their proficiencies. They may do so some of the time. Rather, it means that their probability of success is not as high. In other words, the more difficult the task relative to their proficiency, the lower their likelihood of responding correctly.

The response probabilities for two tasks on the prose scale are displayed in Figure 3.1. The difficulty of the first task is measured at the 250 point on the scale, and the second task is at the 350 point. This means that an individual would have to score at the 250 point on the prose scale to have an 80 percent chance (that is, a .8 probability) of responding correctly to Task 1. Adults scoring at the 200 point on the prose scale have only a 40 percent chance of responding correctly to this task, whereas those scoring at the 300 point and above would be expected to rarely miss this task and others like it.

In contrast, an individual would need to score at the 350 point to have an 80 percent chance of responding correctly to Task 2. While individuals performing at the 250 point would have an 80 percent chance of success on the first task, their probability of answering the more difficult second task correctly is only 20 percent. An individual scoring at the 300 point is likely to succeed on this more difficult task only half the time.

 Figure 3.1

Probabilities of Successful Performance on Two Prose Tasks by Individuals at Selected Points on the Prose Scale

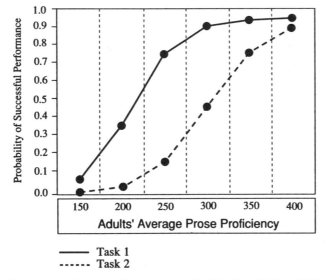

Source: U.S. Department of Education, National Center for Education Statistics, National Adult Literacy Survey, 1992.

An analogy may help clarify the information presented for the two prose tasks. The relationship between task difficulty and individual proficiency is much like the high jump event in track and field, in which an athlete tries to jump over a bar that is placed at increasing heights. Each high jumper has a height at which he or she is proficient. That is, he or she is able to clear the bar at that height with a high probability of success, and can clear the bar at lower levels almost every time. When the bar is higher than their level of proficiency, however, they can be expected to have a much lower chance of clearing it successfully.

Once the literacy tasks are placed on their respective scales, using the criterion described here, it is possible to see how well the interactions among the task characteristics explain the placement of various tasks along the scales.[1] In investigating the progression of task characteristics across the scales, certain questions are of interest. Do tasks with similar difficulty values (that is, with difficulty values near one another on a scale) have certain shared characteristics? Do these characteristics differ in systematic ways from tasks in either higher or lower levels of difficulty? Analyses of the interactions between the materials read and the tasks based on these materials reveal that an ordered set of information-processing skills appears to be called into play to perform the range of tasks along each scale.

To capture this ordering, each scale was divided into five levels that reflect the progression of information-processing skills and strategies: Level 1 (0 to 225), Level 2 (226 to 275), Level 3 (276 to 325), Level 4 (326 to 375), and Level 5 (376 to 500). These levels were determined not as a result of any statistical property of the scales, but rather as a result of shifts in the skills and strategies required to succeed on various tasks along the scales, from simple to complex.

The remaining pages of this section describe each scale in terms of the nature of the task demands at each of the five levels. After a brief introduction to each scale, sample tasks in each level are presented and the factors contributing to their difficulty are discussed. The aim of these discussions is to give meaning to the scales and to facilitate interpretation of the results provided in the first and second sections of this report.

Interpreting the Literacy Levels

Prose Literacy

The ability to understand and use information contained in various kinds of textual material is an important aspect of literacy. Most of the prose materials administered in this assessment were expository — that is, they inform, define, or describe — since these constitute much of the prose that adults read. Some narrative texts and poems were included, as well. The prose materials were drawn from newspapers, magazines, books, brochures, and pamphlets and reprinted in their entirety, using the typography and layout of the original source. As a result, the materials vary widely in length, density of information,

---

[1] I.S. Kirsch and P.B. Mosenthal. (1990). "Exploring Document Literacy: Variables Underlying the Performance of Young Adults." *Reading Research Quarterly*, 25. pp. 5-30.

and the use of structural or organizational aids such as section or paragraph headings, italic or bold face type, and bullets.

Each prose selection was accompanied by one or more questions or directives which asked the reader to perform specific tasks. These tasks represent three major aspects of information-processing: locating, integrating, and generating. Locating tasks require the reader to find information in the text based on conditions or features specified in the question or directive. The match may be literal or synonymous, or the reader may need to make a text-based inference in order to perform the task successfully. Integrating tasks ask the reader to compare or contrast two or more pieces of information from the text. In some cases the information can be found in a single paragraph, while in others it appears in different paragraphs or sections. In the generating tasks, readers must produce a written response by making text-based inferences or drawing on their own background knowledge.

In all, the prose literacy scale includes 41 tasks with difficulty values ranging from 149 to 468. It is important to remember that the locating, generating, and integrating tasks extend over a range of difficulty as a result of interactions with other variables including:

- the number of categories or features of information that the reader must process

- the number of categories or features of information in the text that can distract the reader, or that may seem plausible but are incorrect

- the degree to which information given in the question is obviously related to the information contained in the text

- the length and density of the text

The five levels of prose literacy are defined, and sample tasks provided, in the following pages.

Prose Level 1   Scale range: 0 to 225

Most of the tasks in this level require the reader to read relatively short text to locate a single piece of information which is identical to or synonymous with the information given in the question or directive. If plausible but incorrect information is present in the text, it tends not to be located near the correct information.

Average difficulty value of tasks in this level: 198
Percentage of adults performing in this level: 21%

Tasks in this level require the reader to locate and match a single piece of information in the text. Typically the match between the question or directive and the text is literal, although sometimes synonymous matches may be necessary. The text is usually brief or has organizational aids such as paragraph headings or italics that suggest where in the text the reader should search for the specified information. The word or phrase to be matched appears only once in the text.

One task in Level 1 with a difficulty value of 210 asks respondents to read a newspaper article about a marathon swimmer and to underline the sentence that tells what she ate during a swim. Only one reference to food is contained in the passage, and it does not use the word "ate." Rather, the article says the swimmer "kept up her strength with banana and honey sandwiches, hot chocolate, lots of water and granola bars." The reader must match the word "ate" in the directive with the only reference to foods in the article.

Underline the sentence that tells what Ms. Chanin ate during the swim.

Swimmer completes Manhattan marathon

The Associated Press

NEW YORK—University of Maryland senior Stacy Chanin on Wednesday became the first person to swim three 28-mile laps around Manhattan.

Chanin, 23, of Virginia, climbed out of the East River at 96th Street at 9:30 p.m. She began the swim at noon on Tuesday.

A spokesman for the swimmer, Roy Brunett, said Chanin had kept up her strength with "banana and honey" sandwiches, hot chocolate, lots of water and granola bars."

Chanin has twice circled Manhattan before and trained for the new feat by swimming about 28.4 miles a week. The Yonkers native has competed as a swimmer since she was 15 and hoped to persuade Olympic authorities to add a long-distance swimming event.

The Leukemia Society of America solicited pledges for each mile she swam.

In July 1983, Julie Ridge became the first person to swim around Manhattan twice. With her three laps, Chanin came up just short of Diana Nyad's distance record, set on a Florida-to-Cuba swim.

Reduced from original copy.

Some tasks in this level require readers to locate a single piece of information in the text; however, several distractors or plausible but incorrect pieces of information may be present, or low-level inferences may be required. Other tasks require the reader to integrate two or more pieces of information or to compare and contrast easily identifiable information based on a criterion provided in the question or directive.

Average difficulty value of tasks in this level: 259
Percentage of adults performing in this level: 27%

Like the tasks in Level 1, most of the tasks in this level ask the reader to locate information. However, these tasks place more varied demands on the reader. For example, they frequently require readers to match more than a single piece of information in the text and to discount information that only partially satisfies the question. If plausible but incomplete information is included in the text, such distractors do not appear near the sentence or paragraph that contains the correct answer. For example, a task based on the sports article reproduced earlier asks the reader to identify the age at which the marathon swimmer began to swim competitively. The article first provides the swimmer's current age of 23, which is a plausible but incorrect answer. The correct information, age 15, is found toward the end of the article.

In addition to directing the reader to locate more than a single piece of information in the text, low-level inferences based on the text may be required to respond correctly. Other tasks in Level 2 (226 to 275) require the reader to identify information that matches a given criterion. For example, in one task with a difficulty value of 275, readers were asked to identify specifically what was wrong with an appliance by choosing the most appropriate of four statements describing its malfunction.

A manufacturing company provides its customers with the following instructions for returning appliances for service:

> When returning appliance for servicing, include a note telling as clearly and as specifically as possible what is wrong with the appliance.

A repair person for the company receives four appliances with the following notes attached. Circle the letter next to the note which best follows the instructions supplied by the company.

A
> The clock does not run correctly on this clock radio. I tried fixing it, but I couldn't.

C
> The alarm on my clock radio doesn't go off at the time I set. It rings 15-30 minutes later.

B
> My clock radio is not working. It stopped working right after I used it for five days.

D
> This radio is broken. Please repair and return by United Parcel Service to the address on my slip.

Readers in this level may also be asked to infer a recurring theme. One task with a difficulty value of 262 asks respondents to read a poem that uses several metaphors to represent a single, familiar concept and to identify its theme. The repetitiveness and familiarity of the allusions appear to make this "generating" task relatively easy.

Tasks in this level tend to require readers to make literal or synonymous matches between the text and information given in the task, or to make matches that require low-level inferences. Other tasks ask readers to integrate information from dense or lengthy text that contains no organizational aids such as headings. Readers may also be asked to generate a response based on information that can be easily identified in the text. Distracting information is present, but is not located near the correct information.

Average difficulty value of tasks in this level: 298
Percentage of adults performing in this level: 32%

One of the easier Level 3 tasks requires the reader to write a brief letter explaining that an error has been made on a credit card bill. This task is at 288 on the prose scale. Other tasks in this level require the reader to search fairly dense text for information. Some of the tasks ask respondents to make a literal or synonymous match on more than a single feature, while other tasks ask them to integrate multiple pieces of information from a long passage that does not contain organizational aids.

One of the more difficult Level 3 tasks (with a difficulty value of 316) requires the reader to read a magazine article about an Asian-American woman and to provide two facts that support an inference made from the text. The question directs the reader to identify what Ida Chen did to help resolve conflicts due to discrimination.

List two things that Chen became involved in or has done to help resolve conflicts due to discrimination.

IDA CHEN is the first Asian-American woman to become a judge of the Commonwealth of Pennsylvania.

She understands discrimination because she has experienced it herself.

Soft-spoken and eminently dignified, Judge Ida Chen prefers hearing about a new acquaintance rather than talking about herself. She wants to know about career plans, hopes, dreams, fears. She gives unsolicited advice as well as encouragement. She instills confidence.

Her father once hoped that she would become a professor. And she would have also made an outstanding social worker or guidance counselor. The truth is that Chen wears the caps of all these professions as a Family Court judge of the Court of Common Pleas of Philadelphia County, as a participant in public advocacy for minorities, and as a particularly sensitive, caring person.

She understands discrimination because she has experienced it herself. As an elementary school student, Chen tried to join the local Brownie troop. "You can't be a member," she was told. "Only American girls are in the Brownies."

Originally intent upon a career as a journalist, she selected Temple University because of its outstanding journalism department and affordable tuition. Independence being a personal need, she paid for her tuition by working for Temple's Department of Criminal Justice. There she had her first encounter with the legal world and it turned her career plans in a new direction — law school.

Through meticulous planning, Chen was able to earn her undergraduate degree in two and a half years and she continued to work three jobs. But when she began her first semester as a Temple law student in the fall of 1973, she was barely able to stay awake. Her teacher Lynne Abraham, now a Common Pleas Court judge herself, couldn't help but notice Chen yawning in the back of the class, and when she determined that this student was not a party animal but a workhorse, she arranged a teaching assistant's job for Chen on campus.

After graduating from Temple Law School in 1976, Chen worked for the U.S. Equal Employment Opportunity Commission where she was a litigator on behalf of plaintiffs who experienced discrimination in the workplace, and then moved on to become the first Asian-American to serve on the Philadelphia Commission on Human Relations.

Appointed by Mayor Wilson Goode, Chen worked with community leaders to resolve racial and ethnic tensions and also made time to contribute free legal counsel to a variety of activist groups.

The "Help Wanted" section of the newspaper contained an entry that aroused Chen's curiosity — an ad for a judge's position. Her application resulted in her selection by a state judicial committee to fill a seat in the state court. And in July of 1988, she officially became a judge of the Court of Common Pleas. Running as both a Republican and Democratic candidate, her position was secured when she won her seat on the bench at last November's election.

At Family Court, Chen presides over criminal and civil cases which include adult sex crimes, domestic violence, juvenile delinquency, custody, divorce and support. Not a pretty picture.

Chen recalls her first day as judge, hearing a juvenile dependency case — "It was a horrifying experience. I broke down because the cases were so depressing," she remembers.

Outside of the courtroom, Chen has made a name for herself in resolving interracial conflicts, while glorying in her Chinese-American identity. In a 1986 incident involving the desecration of Korean street signs in a Philadelphia neighborhood, Chen called for a meeting with the leaders of that community to help resolve the conflict.

Chen's interest in community advocacy is not limited to Asian communities. She has been involved in Hispanic, Jewish and Black issues, and because of her participation in the Ethnic Affairs Committee of the Anti-Defamation League of B'nai B'rith, Chen was one of 10 women nationwide selected to take part in a mission to Israel.

With her recently won mandate to judicate in the affairs of Pennsylvania's citizens, Chen has pledged to work tirelessly to defend the rights of its people and contribute to the improvement of human welfare. She would have made a fabulous Brownie.

— *Jessica Schultz*

These tasks require readers to perform multiple-feature matches and to integrate or synthesize information from complex or lengthy passages. More complex inferences are needed to perform successfully. Conditional information is frequently present in tasks in this level and must be taken into consideration by the reader.

Average difficulty value of tasks in this level: 352
Percentage of adults performing in this level: 17%

A prose task with a difficulty value of 328 requires the reader to synthesize the repeated statements of an argument from a newspaper column in order to generate a theme or organizing principle. In this instance, the supporting statements are elaborated in different parts of a lengthy text.

A more challenging task (with a difficulty value of 359) directs the reader to contrast the two opposing views stated in the newspaper feature reprinted here that discusses the existence of technologies that can be used to produce more fuel-efficient cars.

Contrast Dewey's and Hanna's views about the existence of technologies that can be used to produce more fuel-efficient cars while maintaining the size of the cars.

Face-Off: Getting More Miles Per Gallon

Demand cars with better gas mileage

By Robert Dewey
Guest columnist

WASHINGTON — Warning: Automakers are resurrecting their heavy-metal dinosaurs, aka gas guzzlers.

Government reports show that average new-car mileage has declined to 28.2 miles per gallon — the 1986 level. To reverse this trend, Congress must significantly increase existing gas-mileage standards.

More than half our Nobel laureates and 700 members of the National Academy of Sciences recently called global warming "the most serious environmental threat of the 21st century." In 1989, oil imports climbed to a near-record 46% of U.S. consumption. Increasing gas mileage is the single biggest step we can take to reduce oil imports and curb global warming. Greater efficiency also lowers our trade deficit (oil imports represent 40% of it) and decreases the need to drill in pristine areas.

Bigger engines and bigger cars mean bigger profits for automakers, who offer us the products they want us to buy. More than ever, Americans want products that have less of an environmental impact. But with only a few fuel-efficient cars to choose from, how do we find ones that meet all our needs?

Government studies show automakers have the technology to dramatically improve gas mileage — while maintaining the 1987 levels of comfort, performance and size mix of vehicles. Automakers also have the ability to make their products safer. The cost of these improvements will be offset by savings at the gas pump!

Cars can average 45 mpg and light trucks 35 mpg primarily by utilizing engine and transmission technologies already on a few cars today. Further improvements are possible by using technologies like the two-stroke engine and better aerodynamics that have been developed but not used.

When the current vehicle efficiency standards were proposed in 1974, Ford wrongly predicted that they "would require either all sub-Pinto-sized vehicles or some mix of vehicles ranging from a sub-subcompact to perhaps a Maverick." At that time, Congress required a 100% efficiency increase; raising gas mileage to 45 mpg requires only a 60% increase.

Americans want comfortable, safe and efficient cars. If automakers won't provide them, Congress must mandate them when it considers the issue this summer.

Let's hope lawmakers put the best interest of the environment and the nation ahead of the automakers' lobbyists and political action committees.

Robert Dewey is a conservation analyst for the Environmental Action Foundation.

Reprinted by permission of USA Today.

Don't demand end to cars people want

By Thomas H. Hanna
Guest columnist

DETROIT — Do Americans look forward to the day when they'll have to haul groceries, shuttle the kids to and from school or take family vacations in compact and subcompact cars?

I doubt it — which is why U.S. and import carmakers oppose the 40-miles-per-gallon corporate average fuel economy mandates that some are pushing in Congress, either to curb tailpipe carbon dioxide emissions because of alleged global warming or for energy conservation.

Since the mid-1970s, automakers have doubled the fleet average fuel economy of new cars to 28 mpg — and further progress will be made.

Compact and subcompact cars with mileage of 40 mpg or better are now available, yet they appeal to only 5% of U.S. car buyers.

But to achieve a U.S. fleet average of 40 mpg to 45 mpg, carmakers would have to sharply limit the availability of family-size models and dramatically trim the size and weight of most cars.

There simply are not magic technologies to meet such a standard.

Almost every car now sold in the USA would have to be drastically downsized, and many would be obsolete.

As a result, Americans each year would be unable to buy the vehicles most suited for their needs: mid- and family-size models, luxury automobiles, mini-vans, small trucks and utility vehicles.

The fleet shift to compacts and subcompacts could also force the closing of assembly plants, supplier firms and dealerships, at a cost of thousands of U.S. jobs.

Although a growing number of scientists are skeptical of global warming, the issue deserves thorough international scientific evaluation, not premature unilateral U.S. action.

Carbon dioxide emissions from U.S. vehicles total less than 2.5% of worldwide "greenhouse" gases. Even doubling today's corporate average fuel economy for U.S. cars — if technically possible — would cut those gases about .5%

Whatever the motivation — alleged global warming or energy conservation — the stakes are high for millions of Americans and thousands of U.S. jobs in unrealistic corporate average fuel economy mandates.

Thomas H. Hanna is president and chief executive officer of the Motor Vehicle Manufacturers Association of the United States.

Reprinted by permission of USA Today.

Reduced from original copy.

Two other tasks in Level 4 on the prose scale require the reader to draw on background knowledge in responding to questions asked about two poems. In one they are asked to generate an unfamiliar theme from a short poem (difficulty value of 362), and in the other they are asked to compare two metaphors (value of 374).

Prose Level 5   Scale range: 376 to 500

Some tasks in this level require the reader to search for information in dense text which contains a number of plausible distractors. Others ask readers to make high-level inferences or use specialized background knowledge. Some tasks ask readers to contrast complex information.

Average difficulty value of tasks in this level: 423
Percentage of adults performing in this level: 3%

Two tasks in Level 5 require the reader to search for information in dense text containing several plausible distractors. One such task (difficulty value of 410) requires the respondent to read information about jury selection and service. The question requires the reader to interpret information to identify two ways in which prospective jurors may be challenged.

Identify and summarize the two kinds of challenges
that attorneys use while selecting members of a jury.

DO YOU HAVE A QUESTION?

QUESTION: What is the new program for scheduling jurors?

ANSWER: This is a new way of organizing and scheduling jurors that is being introduced all over the country. The goals of this program are to save money, increase the number of citizens who are summoned to serve and decrease the inconvenience of serving.

The program means that instead of calling jurors for two weeks, jurors now serve only one day, or for the length of one trial if they are selected to hear a case. Jurors who are not selected to hear a case are excused at the end of the day, and their obligations to serve as jurors are fulfilled for three years. The average trial lasts two days once testimony begins.

An important part of what is called the One Day – One Trial program is the "standby" juror. This is a person called to the Courthouse if the number of cases to be tried requires more jurors than originally estimated. Once called to the Courthouse, the standby becomes a "regular" juror, and his or her service is complete at the end of one day or one trial, the same as everyone else.

Q. How was I summoned?

A. The basic source for names of eligible jurors is the Driver's License list which is supplemented by the voter registration list. Names are chosen from these combined lists by a computor in a completely random manner.

Once in the Courthouse, jurors are selected for a trial by this same computer and random selection process.

Q. How is the Jury for a particular trial selected?

A. When a group of prospective jurors is selected, more than the number needed for a trial are called. Once this group has been seated in the courtroom, either the Judge or the attorneys ask questions. This is called *voir dire*. The purpose of questions asked during *voir dire* is to ensure that all of the jurors who are selected to hear the case will be unbiased, objective and attentive.

In most cases, prospective jurors will be asked to raise their hands when a particular question applies to them. Examples of questions often asked are: Do you know the Plaintiff, Defendant or the attorneys in this case? Have you been involved in a case similar to this one yourself? Where the answer is yes, the jurors raising hands may be asked additional questions, as the purpose is to guarantee a fair trial for all parties. When an attorney believes that there is a legal reason to excuse a juror, he or she will challenge the juror for cause. Unless both attorneys agree that the juror should be excused, the Judge must either sustain or override the challenge.

After all challenges for cause have been ruled upon, the attorneys will select the trial jury from those who remain by exercising peremptory challenges. Unlike challenges for cause, no reason need be given for excusing a juror by peremptory challenge. Attorneys usually exercise these challenges by taking turns striking names from a list until both are satisfied with the jurors at the top of the list or until they use up the number of challenges allowed. Challenged jurors and any extra jurors will then be excused and asked to return to the jury selection room.

Jurors should not feel rejected or insulted if they are excused for cause by the Court or peremptorily challenged by one of the attorneys. The *voir dire* process and challenging of jurors is simply our judicial system's way of guaranteeing both parties to a lawsuit a fair trial.

Q. Am I guaranteed to serve on a jury?

A. Not all jurors who are summoned actually hear a case. Sometimes all the Judges are still working on trials from the previous day, and no new jurors are chosen. Normally, however, some new cases begin every day. Sometimes jurors are challenged and not selected.

A somewhat more demanding task (difficulty value of 423) involves the magazine article on Ida Chen reproduced earlier. This more challenging task requires the reader to explain the phrase "recently won mandate" used at the end of the text. To explain this phrase, the reader needs to understand the concept of a political mandate as it applies to Ida Chen and the way she is portrayed in this article.

Document Literacy

Another important aspect of being literate in modern society is having the knowledge and skills needed to process information from documents. We often encounter tables, schedules, charts, graphs, maps, and forms in everyday life, both at home and at work. In fact, researchers have found that many of us spend more time reading documents than any other type of material.[2] The ability to locate and use information from documents is therefore essential.

Success in processing documents appears to depend at least in part on the ability to locate information in complex arrays and to use this information in the appropriate ways. Procedural knowledge may be needed to transfer information from one source or document to another, as is necessary in completing applications or order forms.

The NALS document literacy scale contains 81 tasks with difficulty values that range from 69 to 396 on the scale. By examining tasks associated with various proficiency levels, we can identify characteristics that appear to make certain types of document tasks more or less difficult for readers. Questions and directives associated with these tasks are basically of four types: *locating, cycling, integrating,* and *generating.* Locating tasks require the readers to match one or more features of information stated in the question to either identical or synonymous information given in the document. Cycling tasks require the reader to locate and match one or more features, but differ in that they require the reader to engage in a series of feature matches to satisfy conditions given in the question. The integrating tasks typically require the reader to compare and contrast information in adjacent parts of the document. In the generating tasks, readers must produce a written response by processing information found in the document and also making text-based inferences or drawing on their own background knowledge.

---

[2] J.T. Guthrie, M. Seifert, and I.S. Kirsch. (1986). "Effects of Education, Occupation, and Setting on Reading Practices." *American Educational Research Journal,* 23. pp. 151-160.

As with the prose tasks, each type of question or directive extends over a range of difficulty as a result of interactions among several variables or task characteristics that include:

- the number of categories or features of information in the question that the reader has to process or match

- the number of categories or features of information in the document that can serve to distract the reader or that may seem plausible but are incorrect

- the extent to which the information asked for in the question is obviously related to the information stated in the document and

- the structure of the document

A more detailed discussion of the five levels of document literacy is provided in the following pages.

Document Level 1   Scale range: 0 to 225

Tasks in this level tend to require the reader either to locate a piece of information based on a literal match or to enter information from personal knowledge onto a document. Little, if any, distracting information is present.

Average difficulty value of tasks in this level: 195
Percentage of adults performing in this level: 23%

Some of the Level 1 tasks require the reader to match one piece of information in the directive with an identical or synonymous piece of information in the document. For example, readers may be asked to write a piece of personal background information — such as their name or age — in the appropriate place on a document. One task with a difficulty value of 69 directs individuals to look at a Social Security card and sign their name on the line marked "signature." Tasks such as this are quite simple, since only one piece of information is required, it is known to the respondent, and there is only one logical place on the document where it may be entered.

Here is a Social Security card. Sign your name on the line that reads "signature."

SOCIAL SECURITY
ACCOUNT NUMBER
301-02-0304
HAS BEEN ESTABLISHED FOR

SIGNATURE
FOR SOCIAL SECURITY PURPOSES • NOT FOR IDENTIFICATION

Other tasks in this level are slightly more complex. For example, in one task, readers were asked to complete a section of a job application by providing several pieces of information. This was more complicated than the previous task described, since respondents had to conduct a series of one-feature matches. As a result, the difficulty value of this task was higher (218).

You have gone to an employment center for help in finding a job. You know that this center handles many different kinds of jobs. Also, several of your friends who have applied here have found jobs that appeal to you.

The agent has taken your name and address and given you the rest of the form to fill out. Complete the form so the employment center can help you get a job.

Birth date_____ Age____ Sex: Male____ Female____

Height_____ Weight_____ Health_____

Last grade completed in school_____

Kind of work wanted:

    Part-time_____   Summer_____

    Full-time_____   Year-round_____

Other tasks in this level ask the reader to locate specific elements in a document that contains a variety of information. In one task, for example, respondents were given a form providing details about a meeting and asked to indicate the date and time of the meeting, which were stated in the form. The difficulty values associated with these tasks were 183 and 180, respectively. The necessary information was referred to only once in the document.

Document Level 2   Scale range: 226 to 275

Tasks in this level are more varied than those in Level 1. Some require the reader to match a single piece of information; however, several distractors may be present, or the match may require low-level inferences. Tasks in this level may also ask the reader to cycle through information in a document or to integrate information from various parts of a document.

Average difficulty value of tasks in this level: 249
Percentage of adults performing in this level: 28%

Some tasks in Level 2 ask readers to match two pieces of information in the text. For example, one task with a difficulty value of 261 directs the respondent to look at a pay stub and to write "the gross pay for this year to date." To perform the task successfully, respondents must match both "gross pay" and "year to date" correctly. If readers fail to match on both features, they are likely to indicate an incorrect amount.

What is the gross pay for this year to date?

	HOURS			PERIOD ENDING 03/15/85	REGULAR	OVERTIME	GROSS	DEF ANN	NET PAY
REGULAR	2ND SHIFT	OVERTIME	TOTAL	CURRENT	62500		62500		45988
500			500	YEAR TO DATE			426885		

	TAX DEDUCTIONS					OTHER DEDUCTIONS			
	FED W/H	STATE W/H	CITY W/H	FICA	CR UNION	UNITED FD	PERS INS	MISC	MISC CODE
CURRENT	10894	1375		3831					
YEAR TO DATE	73498	8250		26167					

NON-NEGOTIABLE

	OTHER DEDUCTIONS				
CODE	TYPE	AMOUNT	CODE	TYPE	AMOUNT
07	DEN	412			

Reduced from original copy.

A second question based on this document — What is the current net pay? — was also expected to require readers to make a two-feature match. Accordingly, the difficulty values of the two items were expected to be similar. The task anchored at about the 200 point on the scale, however, and an analysis of the pay stub reveals why its difficulty was lower than that of the previous task. To succeed on the second task, the reader only needs to match on the feature "net pay." Since the term appears only once on the pay stub and there is only one number in the column, this task requires only a one-feature match and receives a difficulty value that lies within the Level 1 range on the document scale.

Tasks in Level 2 may also require the reader to integrate information from different parts of the document by looking for similarities or differences. For example, a task with a difficulty value of 268 asks respondents to study a line graph showing a company's seasonal sales over a three-year period, then predict the level of sales for the following year, based on the seasonal trends shown in the graph.

You are a marketing manager for a small manufacturing firm. This graph shows your company's sales over the last three years. Given the seasonal pattern shown on the graph, predict the sales for Spring 1985 (in thousands) by putting an "x" on the graph.

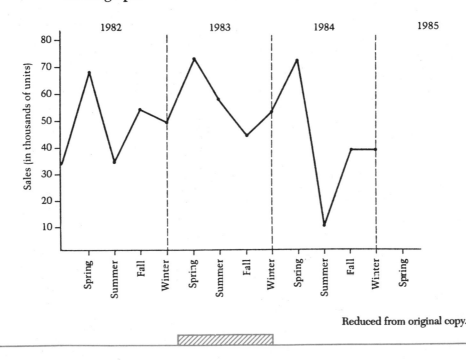

Reduced from original copy.

Some tasks in this level require the reader to integrate multiple pieces of information from one or more documents. Others ask readers to cycle through rather complex tables or graphs which contain information that is irrelevant or inappropriate to the task.

Average difficulty value of tasks in this level: 302
Percentage of adults performing in this level: 31%

Tasks within the range for Level 3 ask the reader to locate particular features in complex displays, such as tables that contain nested information. Typically, distractor information is present in the same row or column as the correct answer. For example, the reader might be asked to use a table that summarizes appropriate uses for a variety of products, and then choose which product to use for a certain project. One such task had a difficulty value of 305. To perform this task successfully, the respondent uses a table containing nested information to determine the type of sandpaper to buy if one needs "to smooth wood in preparation for sealing and plans to buy garnet sandpaper." This task requires matching not only on more than a single feature of information but also on features that are not always superordinate categories in the document. For example, "preparation for sealing" is subordinated or nested under the category "wood," while the type of sandpaper is under the main heading of "garnet." In addition, there are three other types of sandpaper that the reader might select that partially satisfy the directive.

You need to smooth wood in preparation for sealing and plan to buy garnet sandpaper. What type of sandpaper should you buy?

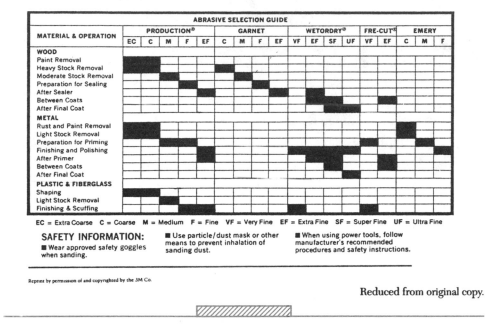

ABRASIVE SELECTION GUIDE

MATERIAL & OPERATION	PRODUCTION®					GARNET				WETORDRY®				FRE-CUT®		EMERY		
	EC	C	M	F	EF	C	M	F	EF	VF	EF	SF	UF	VF	EF	C	M	F
WOOD																		
Paint Removal																		
Heavy Stock Removal																		
Moderate Stock Removal																		
Preparation for Sealing																		
After Sealer																		
Between Coats																		
After Final Coat																		
METAL																		
Rust and Paint Removal																		
Light Stock Removal																		
Preparation for Priming																		
Finishing and Polishing																		
After Primer																		
Between Coats																		
After Final Coat																		
PLASTIC & FIBERGLASS																		
Shaping																		
Light Stock Removal																		
Finishing & Scuffing																		

EC = Extra Coarse   C = Coarse   M = Medium   F = Fine   VF = Very Fine   EF = Extra Fine   SF = Super Fine   UF = Ultra Fine

SAFETY INFORMATION:
■ Wear approved safety goggles when sanding.

■ Use particle/dust mask or other means to prevent inhalation of sanding dust.

■ When using power tools, follow manufacturer's recommended procedures and safety instructions.

Reprint by permission of and copyrighted by the 3M Co.

Reduced from original copy.

At the same level of difficulty (306), another task directs the reader to a stacked bar graph depicting estimated power consumption by source for four different years. The reader is asked to select an energy source that will provide more power in the year 2000 than it did in 1971. To succeed on this task, the reader must first identify the correct years and then compare each of the five pairs of energy sources given.

> Document Level 4   Scale range: 326 to 375
>
> *Tasks in this level, like those in the previous levels, ask readers to perform multiple-feature matches, cycle through documents, and integrate information; however, they require a greater degree of inferencing. Many of these tasks require readers to provide numerous responses but do not designate how many responses are needed. Conditional information is also present in the document tasks in this level and must be taken into account by the reader.*
>
> Average difficulty value of tasks in this level: 340
> Percentage of adults performing in this level: 15%

One task in this level (348) combines many of the variables that contribute to difficulty in Level 4. These include: multiple feature matching, complex displays involving nested information, numerous distractors, and conditional information that must be taken into account in order to arrive at a correct response. Using the bus schedule shown here, readers are asked to select the time of the next bus on a Saturday afternoon, if they miss the 2:35 bus leaving Hancock and Buena Ventura going to Flintridge and Academy. Several departure times are given, from which respondents must choose the correct one.

On Saturday afternoon, if you miss the 2:35 bus leaving Hancock and Buena Ventura going to Flintridge and Academy, how long will you have to wait for the next bus?

ROUTE 5 — VISTA GRANDE

This bus line operates Monday through Saturday providing "local" service to most neighborhoods in the northeast section

Buses run thirty minutes apart during the morning and afternoon rush hours Monday through Friday

Buses run one hour apart at all other times of day and Saturday

No Sunday, holiday or night service.

OUTBOUND (from Terminal) / INBOUND (toward Terminal)

You can transfer from this bus to another headed anywhere else in the city bus system

Leave Downtown Terminal	Leave Hancock and Buena Ventura	Leave Citadel	Leave Rustic Hills	Leave North Carefree and Oro Blanco	Arrive Flintridge and Academy	Leave Flintridge and Academy	Leave North Carefree and Oro Blanco	Leave Rustic Hills	Leave Citadel	Leave Hancock and Buena Ventura	Arrive Downtown Terminal
AM											
						6:15	6:27	6:42	6:47	6:57	7:15
						6:45	6:57	7:12	7:17	7:27	7:45 Monday through Friday only
6:20	6:35	6:45	6:50	7:03	7:15	7:15	7:27	7:42	7:47	7:57	8:15
6:50	7:05	7:15	7:20	7:33	7:45	7:45	7:57	8:12	8:17	8:27	8:45 Monday through Friday only
7:20	7:35	7:45	7:50	8:03	8:15	8:15	8:27	8:42	8:47	8:57	9:15
7:50	8:05	8:15	8:20	8:33	8:45	8:45	8:57	9:12	9:17	9:27	9:45 Monday through Friday only
8:20	8:35	8:45	8:50	9:03	9:15	9:15	9:27	9:42	9:47	9:57	10:15
8:50	9:05	9:15	9:20	9:33	9:45	9:45	9:57	10:12	10:17	10:27	10:45 Monday through Friday only
9:20	9:35	9:45	9:50	10:03	10:15	10:15	10:27	10:42	10:47	10:57	11:15
10:20	10:35	10:45	10:50	11:03	11:15	11:15	11:27	11:42	11:47	11:57	12:15
11:20	11:35	11:45	11:50	12:03	12:15	12:15	12:27	12:42 p.m.	12:47 p.m.	12:57 p.m.	1:15 p.m.
PM											
12:20	12:35	12:45	12:50	1:03	1:15	1:15	1:27	1:42	1:47	1:57	2:15
1:20	1:35	1:45	1:50	2:03	2:15	2:15	2:27	2:42	2:47	2:57	3:15
2:20	2:35	2:45	2:50	3:03	3:15	3:15	3:27	3:42	3:47	3:57	4:15
2:50	3:05	3:15	3:20	3:33	3:45	3:45	3:57	4:12	4:17	4:27	4:45 Monday through Friday only
3:20	3:35	3:45	3:50	4:03	4:15	4:15	4:27	4:42	4:47	4:57	5:15
3:50	4:05	4:15	4:20	4:33	4:45	4:45	4:57	5:12	5:17	5:27	5:45 Monday through Friday only
4:20	4:35	4:45	4:50	5:03	5:15	5:15	5:27	5:42	5:47	5:57	6:15
4:50	5:05	5:15	5:20	5:33	5:45	5:45	5:57	6:12	6:17	6:27	6:45 Monday through Friday only
5:20	5:35	5:45	5:50	6:03	6:15						
5:50	6:05	6:15	6:20	6:33	6:45						Monday through Friday only
6:20	6:35	6:45	6:50	7:03	7:15						

To be sure of a smooth transfer tell the driver of this bus the name of the second bus you need.

Other tasks involving this bus schedule are found in Level 3. These tasks require the reader to match on fewer features of information and do not involve the use of conditional information.

A task receiving a difficulty value of 396 involves reading and understanding a table depicting the results from a survey of parents and teachers evaluating parental involvement in their school. Respondents were asked to write a brief paragraph summarizing the results. This particular task requires readers to integrate the information in the table to compare and contrast the viewpoints of parents and teachers on a selected number of school issues.

Using the information in the table, write a brief paragraph summarizing the extent to which parents and teachers agreed or disagreed on the statements about issues pertaining to parental involvement at their school.

Parents and Teachers Evaluate Parental Involvement at Their School

Do you agree or disagree that ... ?

	Total	Level of School		
		Elementary	Junior High	High School
		percent agreeing		
Our school does a good job of encouraging parental involvement in sports, arts, and other nonsubject areas				
Parents	77	76	74	79
Teachers	77	73	77	85
Our school does a good job of encouraging parental involvement in educational areas				
Parents	73	82	71	64
Teachers	80	84	78	70
Our school only contacts parents when there is a problem with their child				
Parents	55	46	62	63
Teachers	23	18	22	33
Our school does not give parents the opportunity for any meaningful roles				
Parents	22	18	22	28
Teachers	8	8	12	7

Source: The Metropolitan Life Survey of the American Teacher, 1987

Quantitative Literacy

Since adults are often required to perform numerical operations in everyday life, the ability to perform quantitative tasks is another important aspect of literacy. These abilities may seem, at first glance, to be fundamentally different from the types of skills involved in reading prose and documents and, therefore, to extend the concept of literacy beyond its traditional limits. However, research indicates that the processing of printed information plays a critical role in affecting the difficulty of tasks along this scale.[3]

---

[3] I.S. Kirsch and A. Jungeblut. (1986). *Literacy: Profiles of America's Young Adults, Final Report*. Princeton, NJ: Educational Testing Service. I.S. Kirsch, A. Jungeblut, and A. Campbell. (1992). *Beyond the School Doors: The Literacy Needs of Job Seekers Served by the U.S. Department of Labor*. Princeton, NJ: Educational Testing Service.

The NALS quantitative literacy scale contains some 39 tasks with difficulty values that range from 191 to 436. The difficulty of these tasks appears to be a function of several factors, including:

- the particular arithmetic operation called for
- the number of operations needed to perform the task
- the extent to which the numbers are embedded in printed materials and
- the extent to which an inference must be made to identify the type of operation to be performed

In general, it appears that many individuals can perform simple arithmetic operations when both the numbers and operations are made explicit. However, when the numbers to be used must be located in and extracted from different types of documents that contain similar but irrelevant information, or when the operations to be used must be inferred from printed directions, the tasks become increasingly difficult.

A detailed discussion of the five levels of quantitative literacy is provided on the following pages.

Quantitative Level 1   Scale range: 0 to 225

Tasks in this level require readers to perform single, relatively simple arithmetic operations, such as addition. The numbers to be used are provided and the arithmetic operation to be performed is specified.

Average difficulty value of tasks in this level: 206
Percentage of adults performing in this level: 22%

The least demanding task on the quantitative scale (191) requires the reader to total two numbers on a bank deposit slip. In this task, both the numbers and the arithmetic operation are judged to be easily identified and the operation involves the simple addition of two decimal numbers that are set up in column format.

You wish to use the automatic teller machine at your bank to make a deposit. Figure the total amount of the two checks being deposited. Enter the amount on the form in the space next to TOTAL.

Availability of Deposits

Funds from deposits may not be available for immediate withdrawal. Please refer to your institution's rules governing funds availability for details.

Crediting of deposits and payments is subject to verification and collection of actual amounts deposited or paid in accordance with the rules and regulations of your financial institution.

PLEASE PRINT

YOUR MAC CARD NUMBER (No PINs PLEASE)
111   222   333 4

YOUR FINANCIAL INSTITUTION
Union Bank

YOUR ACCOUNT NUMBER
987   555   674

YOUR NAME
Chris Jones

CHECK ONE   ☐ DEPOSIT
                 or
             ☐ PAYMENT

CASH	$	00
LIST CHECKS BY BANK NO.	ENDORSE WITH NAME & ACCOUNT NUMBER	
	557	19
	75	00
TOTAL		

DO NOT DETACH TICKET

DO NOT FOLD   NO COINS OR PAPER CLIPS PLEASE

Quantitative Level 2   Scale range: 226 to 275

Tasks in this level typically require readers to perform a single operation using numbers that are either stated in the task or easily located in the material. The operation to be performed may be stated in the question or easily determined from the format of the material (for example, an order form).

Average difficulty value of tasks in this level: 251
Percentage of adults performing in this level: 25%

In the easier tasks in Level 2, the quantities are also easy to locate. In one such task at 250 on the quantitative scale, the cost of a ticket and bus is given for each of two shows. The reader is directed to determine how much less attending one show will cost in comparison to the other.

The price of one ticket and bus for "Sleuth" costs
how much less than the price of one ticket and bus
for "On the Town"?

THEATER TRIP

A charter bus will leave from the bus stop (near the Conference Center)
at 4 p.m., giving you plenty of time for dinner in New York. Return trip
will start from West 45th Street directly following the plays. Both theaters
are on West 45th Street. Allow about 1½ hours for the return trip.

Time: 4 p.m., Saturday, November 20
Price: "On the Town"   Ticket and bus $11.00
       "Sleuth"   Ticket and bus $8.50
Limit: Two tickets per person

In a more complex set of tasks, the reader is directed to complete an order
form for office supplies using a page from a catalogue. No other specific
instructions as to what parts of the form should be completed are given in the
directive. One task (difficulty value of 270) requires the reader to use a table on
the form to locate the appropriate shipping charges based on the amount of a
specified set of office supplies, to enter the correct amount on an order form,
and then to calculate the total price of the supplies.

Quantitative Level 3   Scale range: 276 to 325

*In tasks in this level, two or more numbers are typically needed to
solve the problem, and these must be found in the material. The
operation(s) needed can be determined from the arithmetic relation
terms used in the question or directive.*

Average difficulty value of tasks in this level: 293
Percentage of adults performing in this level: 31%

In general, tasks within the range for Level 3 ask the reader to perform a single operation of addition, subtraction, multiplication, or division. However, the operation is not stated explicitly in the directive or made clear by the format of the document. Instead, it must be inferred from the terms used in the directive. These tasks are also more difficult because the reader must locate the numbers in various parts of the document in order to perform the operation.

From a bar graph showing percentages of population growth for two groups across six periods, a task at the 278 point on the scale directs the reader to calculate the difference between the groups for one of the years.

A more difficult task in Level 3 (321) requires the use of a bus schedule to determine how long it takes to travel from one location to another on a Saturday. To respond correctly, the reader must match on several features of information given in the question to locate the appropriate times.

Suppose that you took the 12:45 p.m. bus from U.A.L.R. Student Union to 17th and Main on a Saturday. According to the schedule, how many minutes is the bus ride?

356–371 0 – 93 – 5 : QL 3

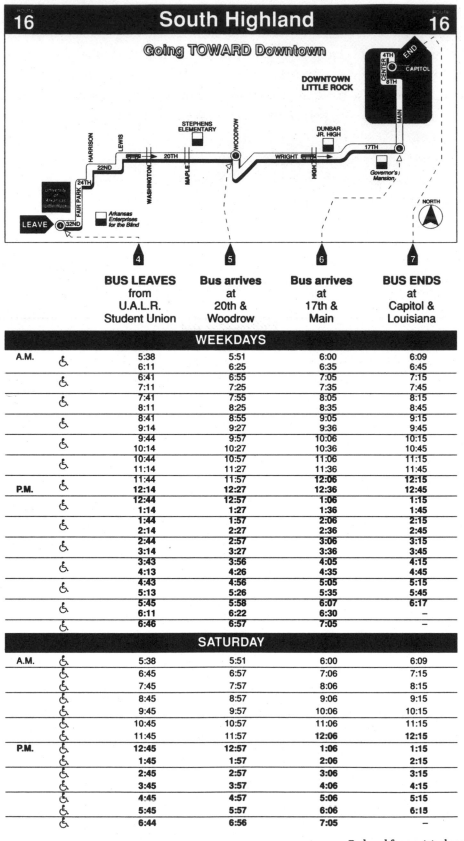

South Highland

ROUTE 16 — ROUTE 16

Going TOWARD Downtown

		4 BUS LEAVES from U.A.L.R. Student Union	5 Bus arrives at 20th & Woodrow	6 Bus arrives at 17th & Main	7 BUS ENDS at Capitol & Louisiana
WEEKDAYS					
A.M.	♿	5:38	5:51	6:00	6:09
		6:11	6:25	6:35	6:45
	♿	6:41	6:55	7:05	7:15
		7:11	7:25	7:35	7:45
	♿	7:41	7:55	8:05	8:15
		8:11	8:25	8:35	8:45
	♿	8:41	8:55	9:05	9:15
		9:14	9:27	9:36	9:45
	♿	9:44	9:57	10:06	10:15
		10:14	10:27	10:36	10:45
	♿	10:44	10:57	11:06	11:15
		11:14	11:27	11:36	11:45
	♿	11:44	11:57	12:06	12:15
P.M.		12:14	12:27	12:36	12:45
	♿	12:44	12:57	1:06	1:15
		1:14	1:27	1:36	1:45
	♿	1:44	1:57	2:06	2:15
		2:14	2:27	2:36	2:45
	♿	2:44	2:57	3:06	3:15
		3:14	3:27	3:36	3:45
	♿	3:43	3:56	4:05	4:15
		4:13	4:26	4:35	4:45
	♿	4:43	4:56	5:05	5:15
		5:13	5:26	5:35	5:45
	♿	5:45	5:58	6:07	6:17
		6:11	6:22	6:30	—
	♿	6:46	6:57	7:05	—
SATURDAY					
A.M.	♿	5:38	5:51	6:00	6:09
	♿	6:45	6:57	7:06	7:15
	♿	7:45	7:57	8:06	8:15
	♿	8:45	8:57	9:06	9:15
	♿	9:45	9:57	10:06	10:15
	♿	10:45	10:57	11:06	11:15
	♿	11:45	11:57	12:06	12:15
P.M.	♿	12:45	12:57	1:06	1:15
	♿	1:45	1:57	2:06	2:15
	♿	2:45	2:57	3:06	3:15
	♿	3:45	3:57	4:06	4:15
	♿	4:45	4:57	5:06	5:15
	♿	5:45	5:57	6:06	6:15
	♿	6:44	6:56	7:05	—

Reduced from original copy.

One task in this level, with a difficulty value of 332, asks the reader to estimate, based on information in a news article, how many miles per day a driver covered in a sled-dog race. The respondent must know that to calculate a "per day" rate requires the use of division.

A more difficult task (355) requires the reader to select from two unit price labels to estimate the cost per ounce of creamy peanut butter. To perform this task successfully, readers may have to draw some information from prior knowledge.

Estimate the cost per ounce of the creamy peanut butter. Write your estimate on the line provided.

Unit price	You pay
11.8¢ per oz.	1.89
rich chnky pnt bt	
10693	16 oz.

Unit price	You pay
1.59 per lb.	1.99
creamy pnt butter	
10732	20 oz.

One of the most difficult tasks on the quantitative scale (433) requires readers to look at an advertisement for a home equity loan and then, using the information given, explain how they would calculate the total amount of interest charges associated with the loan.

You need to borrow $10,000. Find the ad for Home Equity Loans on page 2 in the newspaper provided. Explain to the interviewer how you would compute the total amount of interest charges you would pay under this loan plan. Please tell the interviewer when you are ready to begin.

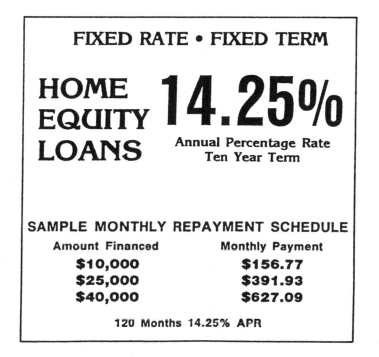

FIXED RATE • FIXED TERM

HOME EQUITY LOANS **14.25%**
Annual Percentage Rate
Ten Year Term

SAMPLE MONTHLY REPAYMENT SCHEDULE

Amount Financed	Monthly Payment
$10,000	$156.77
$25,000	$391.93
$40,000	$627.09

120 Months 14.25% APR

Reduced from original copy.

Estimating Performance Across the Literacy Levels

The literacy levels not only provide a way to explore the progression of information-processing demands across the scales; they can also be used to explore the likelihood that individuals in each level will succeed on tasks of varying difficulty.

The following graphs (FIGURE 3.2) display the probability that individuals performing at selected points on each scale will give a correct response to tasks with varying difficulty values. We see, for example, that a person whose prose proficiency is 150 has less than a 50 percent chance of giving a correct response to the Level 1 tasks. Individuals whose proficiency scores were at the 200 point, on the other hand, have an almost 80 percent probability of responding correctly to these tasks.

In terms of task demands, we can infer that adults performing at the 200 point on the prose scale are likely to be able to locate a single piece of information in a brief piece of text where there is no distracting information, or when any distracting information is located apart from the desired information. They are likely to have far more difficulty with the types of tasks that occur in Levels 2 through 5, however. For example, they would have only about a 30 percent chance of performing the average task in Level 2 correctly and only about a 10 percent chance of success, or less, on the more challenging tasks found in Levels 3, 4, and 5.

In contrast, readers at the 300 point on the prose scale have an 80 percent (or higher) likelihood of success on tasks in Levels 1, 2, and 3. This means that they demonstrate skill identifying information in fairly dense text without organizational aids. They can also integrate, compare, and contrast information that is easily identified in the text. On the other hand, they are likely to have difficulty with tasks that require them to make higher level inferences, to take conditional information into account, and to use specialized knowledge. The probabilities of their performing these Level 4 tasks successfully are just under 50 percent, and on the Level 5 tasks their likelihood of responding correctly falls to under 20 percent.

Average Probabilities of Successful Performance by Individuals with Selected Proficiency Scores on the Tasks in Each Literacy Level

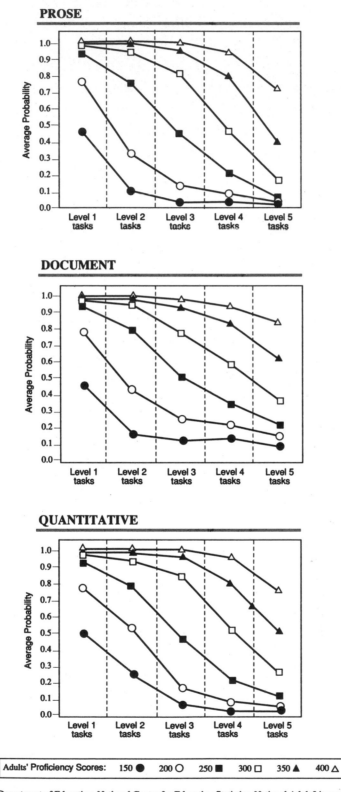

PROSE

DOCUMENT

QUANTITATIVE

Adults' Proficiency Scores: 150 ●   200 ○   250 ■   300 □   350 ▲   400 △

Source: U.S. Department of Education, National Center for Education Statistics, National Adult Literacy Survey, 1992.

Similar interpretations can be made using the performance results on the document and quantitative scales. For example, an individual with a proficiency of 150 on the quantitative scale is estimated to have only a 50 percent chance of responding correctly to tasks in Level 1 and less than a 30 percent chance of responding to tasks in each of the other levels. Such an individual demonstrates little or no proficiency in performing the range of quantitative tasks found in this assessment. In contrast, someone with a proficiency of 300 meets or exceeds the 80 percent criterion for the average tasks in Levels 1, 2, and 3. They can be expected to encounter more difficulty with tasks in Levels 4 and 5.

APPENDICES

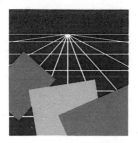

Total Population
The total population includes adults aged 16 and older who participated in the national household survey, the state surveys, and the survey of prisoners.

1985 Young Adult Literacy Survey Population
A national household survey of the literacy skills of young adults (aged 21 to 25) was conducted in 1985. Because the NALS also assessed young adults and readministered a set of tasks, it is possible to compare the literacy skills of individuals assessed in 1985 and those assessed in 1992 — including not only 21- to 25-year-olds but also 28- to 32-year-olds, who were 21 to 25 years of age in 1985.

English Literacy
Respondents were asked two questions about their English literacy skills. One question asked how well they read English, and the other asked how well they write it. Four response options were given: very well, well, not well, and not at all. Adults who answered "very well" or "well" to either question were counted as reporting that they read or write English well. All others were counted as reporting that they do not read or write English well.

Help with Everyday Literacy Tasks
Respondents were asked how much help they get from family members or friends with various types of everyday literacy tasks. Four response options were given: a lot, some, a little, and none. The percentages of adults in each level who reported getting a lot of help with printed information, filling out forms, and using basic arithmetic were analyzed.

Highest Level of Education Completed
Respondents were asked to indicate the highest level of education they completed in this country. The following options were given:

> Still in high school
> Less than high school
> Some high school
> GED or high school equivalency
> High school graduate
> Vocational, trade, or business school after high school
> College: less than 2 years
> College: associate's degree (A.A.)

College: 2 or more years, no degree
College graduate (B.S. or B.A.)
Postgraduate, no degree
Postgraduate degree (M.S., M.A., Ph.D., M.D., etc.)

In one education variable (Education 1), GED recipients and high school graduates were separate groups and the following four groups were created: adults who had completed some postsecondary education but who had not earned a degree, individuals who had earned a two year degree, individuals who had earned a four year degree, and individuals who had completed some graduate work or received a graduate degree. In a second variable (Education 2), GED recipients and high school graduates were combined into one category, and adults who had completed some education beyond high school were divided into two categories: those who had not received a degree and those who had.

Parents' Level of Education

Respondents were asked to indicate the highest level of education completed by their mother (or stepmother or female guardian) and by their father (or stepfather or male guardian). The analyses in this report are based on the highest level of education attained by either parent.

Age

Respondents were asked to report their date of birth, and this information was used to calculate their age. One age variable (Age 1) included the following categories: 16 to 18, 19 to 24, 25 to 39, 40 to 54, 55 to 64, and 65 and older. A second variable (Age 2) included these categories: 16 to 24, 25 to 34, 35 to 44, 45 to 54, 55 to 64, and 65 and older.

Average Years of Schooling

Responses to the question on the highest level of education completed were used to calculate the average number of years of schooling completed. Individuals who were still in school were left out of this analysis. Adults who had not graduated from high school were asked to indicate exactly how many years of schooling they had completed (0 through 12). Individuals who did not provide this information were assigned a value equal to the average number of years of schooling completed by those who did provide this information. For adults in the category "0 to 8 years of education," the average number of years of schooling was 6.10. For adults in the category "9 to 12 years of education," the average number of years of schooling was 10.11. The remaining adults were assigned values representing the number of years of schooling completed, as follows:

GED, high school equivalency	12
High school graduate	12
Vocational, trade, or business school	13
College: less than 2 years	13
College: associate's degree (A.A.)	14
College: 2 or more years, no degree	14.5
College graduate (B.S. or B.A.)	16
Postgraduate, no degree	17
Postgraduate degree	18

Using these values, the average number of years of schooling was calculated for various reporting groups (such as age and race/ethnicity).

Race/Ethnicity

Respondents were asked two questions about their race and ethnicity. One question asked them to indicate which of the following best describes them. The interviewer recorded the races of respondents who refused to answer the question.

White   Pacific Islander
Black (African American)   Asian
American Indian   Other
Alaskan Native

The other question asked respondents to indicate whether they were of Spanish or Hispanic origin or descent. Those who responded "yes" were asked to identify which of the following groups best describes their Hispanic origin:

Mexicano, Mexican, Mexican American, Chicano
Puerto Rican
Cuban
Central/South American
Other Spanish/Hispanic

Adults of Pacific Islander origin were grouped with those of Asian origin, and Alaskan Natives were grouped with American Indians, due to small sample sizes. All other racial/ethnic groups are reported separately. In some analyses, however, the Hispanic subpopulations are combined to provide reliable estimates.

Country of Birth

Respondents were asked to indicate whether they were born in the United States (50 states or Washington, D.C.), a U.S. territory, or another country. Based on their responses, they were divided into two groups: adults born in this country, and those born in another country. Adults who reported they were born in a U.S. territory were counted as being born in another country.

Type of Physical, Mental, or Other Health Condition

Respondents were asked to identify whether they had any of the following:

- a physical, mental, or other health condition that keeps them from participating fully in work, school, housework, or other activities
- difficulty seeing the words or letters in ordinary newspaper print even when wearing glasses or contact lenses, if they usually wear them
- difficulty hearing what is said in a normal conversation with another person even when using a hearing aid, if they usually wear one
- a learning disability
- any mental or emotional condition
- mental retardation
- a speech disability
- a physical disability
- a long-term illness (6 months or more)
- any other health impairment

Respondents were able to indicate each physical, mental, or health condition they had. Thus, these categories are not mutually exclusive.

Region

Census definitions of regions are used in the National Adult Literacy Survey. The four regions analyzed are the Northeast, Midwest, South, and West. The states in each region are identified below.

Northeast: Maine, New Hampshire, Vermont, Massachusetts, Rhode Island, Connecticut, New York, New Jersey, Pennsylvania

Midwest: Ohio, Indiana, Illinois, Michigan, Wisconsin, Minnesota, Iowa, Missouri, North Dakota, South Dakota, Nebraska, Kansas

South: Delaware, Maryland, District of Columbia, Virginia, West Virginia, North Carolina, South Carolina, Georgia, Florida, Kentucky, Tennessee, Alabama, Mississippi, Arkansas, Louisiana, Oklahoma, Texas

West: Montana, Idaho, Wyoming, Colorado, New Mexico, Arizona, Utah, Nevada, Washington, Oregon, California, Alaska, Hawaii

Sex

The interviewers recorded the sex of each respondent.

Prison Population

The incarcerated sample includes only those individuals who were in state or federal prisons at the time of the survey. Those held in local jails, community-based facilities, or other types of institutions were not surveyed.

Voting

The survey asked whether respondents had voted in a national or state election in the past five years. Some participants reported being ineligible to vote, and they were excluded from the analyses. The results reported herein reflect the percentages of adults who voted, of those who were eligible to vote.

Frequency of Newspaper Reading

Respondents were asked how often they read a newspaper in English: every day, a few times a week, once a week, less than once a week, or never.

Newspaper Reading Practices

Respondents were given a list of different parts of the newspaper and asked to identify which parts they generally read. Their responses were grouped as follows:

news, editorial pages, financial news and stock listings

home, fashion, and health sections, and book, movie, or art reviews

classified ads, other ads, and TV, movie, or concert listings

comics, horoscope or advice columns

sports

The responses to this question and the prior question on the frequency of newspaper reading were then combined, to determine the percentage of adults who read the newspaper at least one a week who read various parts.

Sources of Information

Respondents were asked how much information about current events, public affairs, and the government they usually get from newspapers, magazines, radio, television, and family members, friends, or coworkers. The responses to these questions were used to construct a new variable that reflects the extent to which adults get information from different sources:

Print media: Adults who get "some" or "a lot" of information from either newspapers or magazines, and those who do not

Nonprint media: Adults who get "some" or "a lot" of information from either television or radio, and those who do not

Personal sources: Adults who get "some" or "a lot" of information from family, friends, or coworkers, and those who do not

Poverty Status

Respondents were asked to report the number of persons living in their household as well as their family's total income from all sources during the previous calendar year. Their responses to these two questions were used to construct the poverty status variable. Based on the 1991 poverty income thresholds of the federal government, the following criteria were used to identify respondents who were poor or near poor:

Respondents whose family size was:	And whose annual household income was at or below:
1	$ 8,665
2	$11,081
3	$13,575
4	$17,405
5	$20,570
6	$23,234
7	$26,322
8	$29,506
9	$34,927

Sources of Nonwage Income and Support

Respondents were asked to indicate which of the following types of income and support they or anyone in their family received during the past 12 months: Social Security, Supplemental Security Income, retirement payments, Aid to Families with Dependent Children, food stamps, interest from savings or other bank accounts, dividend income, and income from other sources. Each source was treated as a separate variable, and respondents were divided into two groups: those who had received this type of income or support, and those who had not. This report analyzes results for adults who reported receiving food stamps or interest from savings.

Employment Status
Respondents were asked what they were doing the week before the survey:

1) working at a full-time job for pay or profit (35 hours or more)
2) working two or more part-time jobs for pay, totaling 35 or more hours
3) working for pay or profit part time (1 to 35 hours)
4) unemployed, laid off, or looking for work
5) with a job but not at work
6) with a job but on family leave (maternity or paternity leave)
7) in school
8) keeping house
9) retired
10) doing volunteer work

Respondents were then divided into four groups: adults working full time (or working two or more part-time jobs); those working part time; those unemployed, laid off, or looking for work; and those out of the labor force. Adults in categories 1 and 2 above were counted as being employed full time; those in category 2 were counted as being employed part time; those in category 3 were counted as unemployed; those in categories 5 and 6 were counted as being not at work; and those in categories 7 through 10 were counted as being out of the labor force.

Weeks Worked
All respondents, including those who were unemployed or out of the labor force the week before the survey, were asked to indicate how many weeks they worked for pay or profit during the past 12 months, including paid leave (such as vacation and sick leave).

Weekly Wages
Respondents who were employed either full time or part time or were on leave the week before the survey were asked to report their average wage or salary (including tips and commissions) before deductions. They reported their wage or salary per hour, day, week, two-week period, month, year, or other unit of time, and these data were used to calculate their weekly wages.

Occupational Categories
Respondents were asked two questions about their current or most recent job, whether full time or part time. The first question asked them to identify the type of business or industry in which they worked — for example, television manufacturing, retail shoe store, or farm. The second question asked them to indicate their occupation, or the name of their job — for example, electrical engineer, stock clerk, typist, or farmer. Their responses were used to create four occupational categories: management, professional, and technical; sales and clerical; craft and service; and labor, assembly, fishing, and farming.

TABLE 1.1A

Average Prose Proficiency and Literacy Levels by Total Population, Gender, Census Region, and Race/Ethnicity

DEMOGRAPHIC SUBPOPULATIONS	PROSE SCALE		Level 1 225 or lower	Level 2 226 to 275	Level 3 276 to 325	Level 4 326 to 375	Level 5 376 or higher	Overall Proficiency
	n	WGT N (/1,000)	RPCT (SE)	RPCT (SE)	RPCT (SE)	RPCT (SE)	RPCT (SE)	PROF (SE)
Total Population								
Total	26,091	191,289	21 (0.4)	27 (0.6)	32 (0.7)	17 (0.4)	3 (0.2)	272 (0.6)
Gender								
Male	11,770	92,098	22 (0.6)	26 (0.9)	31 (1.2)	18 (0.5)	4 (0.3)	272 (0.9)
Female	14,279	98,901	20 (0.5)	28 (0.7)	33 (0.7)	17 (0.5)	3 (0.2)	273 (0.8)
Census Region								
Northeast	5,425	39,834	22 (0.8)	28 (1.5)	31 (1.1)	16 (0.7)	3 (0.3)	270 (1.1)
Midwest	7,494	45,318	16 (0.8)	28 (1.0)	35 (1.2)	18 (0.7)	3 (0.3)	279 (1.1)
South	7,886	65,854	23 (1.1)	28 (1.1)	30 (0.9)	15 (1.1)	3 (0.3)	267 (1.9)
West	5,286	40,282	20 (1.2)	23 (1.5)	33 (1.5)	21 (1.1)	4 (0.5)	276 (1.8)
Race/Ethnicity								
Black	4,963	21,192	38 (1.1)	37 (1.3)	21 (1.0)	4 (0.5)	0[†](0.1)	237 (1.4)
Hispanic/Mexicano	1,776	10,235	54 (1.9)	25 (1.6)	16 (1.3)	5 (0.8)	0[†](0.3)	206 (3.3)
Hispanic/ Puerto Rican	405	2,190	47 (5.0)	32 (5.5)	17 (3.6)	3 (1.7)	0[†](0.3)	218 (6.1)
Hispanic/Cuban	147	928	53 (6.7)	24 (7.0)	17 (4.2)	6 (4.7)	1 (2.1)	211 (8.7)
Hispanic/ Central/South	424	2,608	56 (3.8)	22 (3.4)	17 (3.9)	4 (1.5)	0[†](0.3)	207 (5.8)
Hispanic/Other	374	2,520	25 (3.2)	27 (5.9)	33 (5.2)	13 (3.4)	2 (1.6)	260 (5.3)
Asian/ Pacific Islander	438	4,116	36 (4.4)	25 (3.8)	25 (3.1)	12 (1.9)	2 (0.7)	242 (6.7)
American Indian/ Alaskan Native	189	1,803	25 (5.9)!	39 (7.1)!	28 (7.3)!	7 (2.9)!	1 (1.5)!	254 (4.1)!
White	17,292	144,968	14 (0.4)	25 (0.6)	36 (0.8)	21 (0.5)	4 (0.3)	286 (0.7)
Other	83	729	53 (9.9)	23 (7.0)	15 (10.7)	9 (4.5)	0[†](0.4)	213 (17.5)

n = sample size; WGT N = population size estimate / 1,000 (the sample sizes for subpopulations may not add up to the total sample sizes, due to missing data); RPCT = row percentage estimate; PROF = average proficiency estimate; (SE) = standard error of the estimate (the reported sample estimate can be said to be within 2 standard errors of the true population value with 95% confidence).

[†] Percentages less than 0.5 are rounded to zero.
! Interpret with caution -- the nature of the sample does not allow accurate determination of the variability of this statistic.

Source: U.S. Department of Education, National Center for Education Statistics, National Adult Literacy Survey, 1992.

TABLE 1.1B

Average Document Proficiency and Literacy Levels by Total Population, Gender, Census Region, and Race/Ethnicity

DEMOGRAPHIC SUBPOPULATIONS	DOCUMENT SCALE		Level 1 225 or lower	Level 2 226 to 275	Level 3 276 to 325	Level 4 326 to 375	Level 5 376 or higher	Overall Proficiency
	n	WGT N (/1,000)	RPCT (SE)	RPCT (SE)	RPCT (SE)	RPCT (SE)	RPCT (SE)	PROF (SE)
Total Population								
Total	26,091	191,289	23 (0.4)	28 (0.5)	31 (0.5)	15 (0.4)	3 (0.2)	267 (0.7)
Gender								
Male	11,770	92,098	23 (0.6)	27 (0.5)	31 (0.8)	17 (0.5)	3 (0.2)	269 (0.9)
Female	14,279	98,901	23 (0.6)	30 (0.7)	31 (0.6)	14 (0.5)	2 (0.2)	265 (0.9)
Census Region								
Northeast	5,425	39,834	24 (0.9)	29 (1.1)	30 (1.1)	14 (1.0)	2 (0.3)	264 (1.2)
Midwest	7,494	45,318	19 (0.8)	30 (1.1)	33 (1.3)	16 (0.9)	2 (0.3)	274 (1.3)
South	7,886	65,854	26 (1.2)	29 (0.8)	29 (1.0)	14 (0.7)	2 (0.3)	262 (1.9)
West	5,286	40,282	22 (1.0)	24 (1.3)	32 (1.2)	18 (1.1)	3 (0.4)	271 (1.6)
Race/Ethnicity								
Black	4,963	21,192	43 (1.0)	36 (1.2)	18 (0.9)	3 (0.4)	0†(0.1)	230 (1.2)
Hispanic/Mexicano	1,776	10,235	54 (2.1)	25 (1.9)	16 (1.6)	4 (0.8)	0†(0.2)	205 (3.5)
Hispanic/ Puerto Rican	405	2,190	49 (3.8)	29 (5.1)	18 (2.6)	3 (1.1)	0†(0.3)	215 (6.6)
Hispanic/Cuban	147	928	48 (8.1)	30 (6.2)	16 (4.3)	4 (3.9)	2 (1.2)	212 (11.3)
Hispanic/ Central/South	424	2,608	53 (3.9)	25 (3.8)	16 (3.6)	4 (1.5)	0†(0.5)	206 (5.5)
Hispanic/Other	374	2,520	28 (3.0)	26 (3.6)	32 (4.4)	12 (4.4)	2 (1.8)	254 (5.3)
Asian/ Pacific Islander	438	4,116	34 (3.5)	25 (3.6)	28 (3.7)	12 (2.3)	2 (0.9)	245 (5.6)
American Indian/ Alaskan Native	189	1,803	27 (4.1)!	37 (5.0)!	29 (5.7)!	7 (3.3)!	0†(0.5)!	254 (4.9)!
White	17,292	144,968	16 (0.5)	27 (0.6)	34 (0.7)	19 (0.5)	3 (0.2)	280 (0.8)
Other	83	729	52 (10.4)	22 (7.6)	15 (6.0)	9 (4.3)	2 (1.8)	213 (15.5)

n = sample size; WGT N = population size estimate / 1,000 (the sample sizes for subpopulations may not add up to the total sample sizes, due to missing data); RPCT = row percentage estimate; PROF = average proficiency estimate; (SE) = standard error of the estimate (the reported sample estimate can be said to be within 2 standard errors of the true population value with 95% confidence).

† Percentages less than 0.5 are rounded to zero.
! Interpret with caution -- the nature of the sample does not allow accurate determination of the variability of this statistic.

Source: U.S. Department of Education, National Center for Education Statistics, National Adult Literacy Survey, 1992.

TABLE 1.1C

Average Quantitative Proficiency and Literacy Levels by Total Population, Gender, Census Region, and Race/Ethnicity

DEMOGRAPHIC SUBPOPULATIONS	QUANTITATIVE SCALE		Level 1 225 or lower	Level 2 226 to 275	Level 3 276 to 325	Level 4 326 to 375	Level 5 376 or higher	Overall Proficiency
	n	WGT N (/1,000)	RPCT (SE)	RPCT (SE)	RPCT (SE)	RPCT (SE)	RPCT (SE)	PROF (SE)
Total Population								
Total	26,091	191,289	22 (0.5)	25 (0.6)	31 (0.6)	17 (0.3)	4 (0.2)	271 (0.7)
Gender								
Male	11,770	92,098	21 (0.7)	23 (0.5)	31 (0.6)	20 (0.4)	5 (0.3)	277 (0.9)
Female	14,279	98,901	23 (0.5)	28 (0.9)	31 (1.0)	15 (0.6)	3 (0.3)	266 (0.9)
Census Region								
Northeast	5,425	39,834	24 (0.8)	25 (0.8)	31 (0.8)	16 (0.6)	4 (0.4)	267 (1.2)
Midwest	7,494	45,318	17 (1.0)	26 (1.5)	34 (1.4)	19 (0.9)	4 (0.3)	280 (1.7)
South	7,886	65,854	25 (1.0)	27 (1.0)	29 (1.1)	15 (0.8)	4 (0.3)	265 (2.0)
West	5,286	40,282	20 (1.0)	22 (0.9)	32 (1.0)	20 (1.0)	5 (0.4)	276 (1.8)
Race/Ethnicity								
Black	4,963	21,192	46 (1.0)	34 (1.1)	17 (1.0)	3 (0.4)	0[†](0.1)	224 (1.4)
Hispanic/Mexicano	1,776	10,235	54 (1.7)	25 (2.0)	17 (2.0)	4 (0.8)	0[†](0.2)	205 (3.6)
Hispanic/ Puerto Rican	405	2,190	51 (3.3)	28 (4.8)	17 (3.2)	3 (1.3)	1 (0.4)	212 (7.2)
Hispanic/Cuban	147	928	46 (6.4)	20 (6.1)	25 (5.2)	6 (5.6)	3 (2.5)	223 (12.9)
Hispanic/ Central/South	424	2,608	53 (3.7)	25 (4.1)	18 (2.8)	4 (1.5)	0[†](0.4)	203 (5.7)
Hispanic/Other	374	2,520	31 (3.0)	25 (4.6)	31 (3.1)	11 (4.7)	1 (0.7)	246 (6.9)
Asian/ Pacific Islander	438	4,116	30 (3.9)	23 (3.4)	27 (3.0)	16 (2.4)	4 (1.7)	256 (6.7)
American Indian/ Alaskan Native	189	1,803	33 (5.6)!	32 (6.1)!	28 (5.9)!	7 (2.9)!	1 (1.0)!	250 (5.1)!
White	17,292	144,968	14 (0.5)	24 (0.6)	35 (0.7)	21 (0.4)	5 (0.2)	287 (0.8)
Other	83	729	49 (8.5)	21 (7.4)	22 (10.1)	6 (4.1)	2 (2.3)	220 (13.1)

n = sample size; WGT N = population size estimate / 1,000 (the sample sizes for subpopulations may not add up to the total sample sizes, due to missing data); RPCT = row percentage estimate; PROF = average proficiency estimate; (SE) = standard error of the estimate (the reported sample estimate can be said to be within 2 standard errors of the true population value with 95% confidence).

[†] Percentages less than 0.5 are rounded to zero.

! Interpret with caution -- the nature of the sample does not allow accurate determination of the variability of this statistic.

Source: U.S. Department of Education, National Center for Education Statistics, National Adult Literacy Survey, 1992.

TABLE 1.2A

Average Prose Proficiency and Literacy Levels by Education Level and Age

EDUCATION LEVEL AND AGE SUBPOPULATIONS	PROSE SCALE		Level 1 225 or lower	Level 2 226 to 275	Level 3 276 to 325	Level 4 326 to 375	Level 5 376 or higher	Overall Proficiency
	n	WGT N (/1,000)	RPCT (SE)	RPCT (SE)	RPCT (SE)	RPCT (SE)	RPCT (SE)	PROF (SE)
Education Level 1								
Still in high school	973	8,268	16 (1.8)	36 (2.2)	37 (2.6)	11 (1.9)	0† (0.5)	271 (2.0)
0 to 8 years	2,167	18,356	75 (1.7)	20 (1.4)	4 (0.9)	0† (0.3)	0† (0.0)	177 (2.6)
9 to 12 years	3,311	24,982	42 (1.4)	38 (1.1)	17 (1.0)	2 (0.4)	0† (0.1)	231 (1.5)
GED	1,062	7,224	14 (1.6)	39 (2.5)	39 (2.8)	7 (1.2)	0† (0.6)	268 (1.8)
High school	6,107	51,290	16 (0.8)	36 (1.3)	37 (1.7)	10 (0.9)	1 (0.2)	270 (1.1)
Some college (no degree)	6,587	39,634	8 (0.5)	23 (0.8)	45 (0.9)	22 (0.8)	3 (0.3)	294 (1.0)
2 year college degree	1,033	6,831	4 (1.1)	19 (2.3)	41 (2.9)	32 (2.5)	4 (0.9)	308 (2.4)
4 year college degree	2,534	17,804	4 (0.7)	11 (1.2)	35 (2.0)	40 (1.5)	10 (1.3)	322 (1.6)
Graduate studies/degree	2,253	16,306	2 (0.4)	7 (1.0)	28 (1.4)	47 (1.8)	16 (1.1)	336 (1.4)
Education Level 2								
Still in high school	973	8,268	16 (1.8)	36 (2.2)	37 (2.6)	11 (1.9)	0† (0.5)	271 (2.0)
0 to 8 years	2,167	18,356	75 (1.7)	20 (1.4)	4 (0.9)	0† (0.3)	0† (0.0)	177 (2.6)
9 to 12 years	3,311	24,982	42 (1.4)	38 (1.1)	17 (1.0)	2 (0.4)	0† (0.1)	231 (1.5)
GED/high school diploma	7,169	58,514	16 (0.7)	36 (1.1)	37 (1.4)	10 (0.8)	1 (0.2)	270 (1.0)
Some college (no degree)	6,587	39,634	8 (0.5)	23 (0.8)	45 (0.9)	22 (0.8)	3 (0.3)	294 (1.0)
College degree (2 or more years)	5,820	40,941	3 (0.4)	11 (0.8)	33 (1.2)	41 (1.2)	12 (0.7)	325 (1.1)
Age 1								
16 to 18 years	1,237	10,424	16 (1.3)	35 (1.9)	38 (2.4)	11 (1.7)	1 (0.4)	271 (1.8)
19 to 24 years	3,344	24,515	14 (1.1)	29 (1.7)	37 (1.8)	18 (1.3)	2 (0.4)	280 (1.3)
25 to 39 years	10,050	63,278	15 (0.5)	24 (0.7)	34 (0.8)	22 (0.8)	5 (0.4)	284 (0.9)
40 to 54 years	6,310	43,794	15 (0.7)	23 (1.0)	34 (1.4)	22 (0.9)	5 (0.4)	286 (1.4)
55 to 64 years	2,924	19,503	26 (1.5)	31 (1.3)	30 (1.5)	12 (1.1)	1 (0.3)	260 (1.9)
65 years and older	2,214	29,735	44 (1.6)	32 (1.6)	19 (1.3)	5 (0.9)	1 (0.3)	230 (2.1)
Age 2								
16 to 24 years	4,581	34,939	15 (0.9)	31 (1.4)	37 (1.4)	16 (1.1)	2 (0.3)	278 (1.0)
25 to 34 years	6,701	41,326	16 (0.7)	25 (1.0)	34 (0.8)	21 (0.9)	4 (0.4)	282 (1.2)
35 to 44 years	5,930	39,755	14 (0.6)	21 (1.0)	35 (1.2)	24 (0.8)	6 (0.5)	289 (1.3)
45 to 54 years	3,729	25,992	16 (0.9)	25 (1.3)	34 (1.6)	21 (1.0)	5 (0.5)	282 (1.7)
55 to 64 years	2,924	19,503	26 (1.5)	31 (1.3)	30 (1.5)	12 (1.1)	1 (0.3)	260 (1.9)
65 years and older	2,214	29,735	44 (1.6)	32 (1.6)	19 (1.3)	5 (0.9)	1 (0.3)	230 (2.1)

n = sample size; WGT N = population size estimate / 1,000 (the sample sizes for subpopulations may not add up to the total sample sizes, due to missing data); RPCT = row percentage estimate; PROF = average proficiency estimate; (SE) = standard error of the estimate (the reported sample estimate can be said to be within 2 standard errors of the true population value with 95% confidence).

† Percentages less than 0.5 are rounded to zero.

Source: U.S. Department of Education, National Center for Education Statistics, National Adult Literacy Survey, 1992.

TABLE 1.2B

Average Document Proficiency and Literacy Levels by Education Level and Age

EDUCATION LEVEL AND AGE SUBPOPULATIONS	DOCUMENT SCALE		Level 1 225 or lower	Level 2 226 to 275	Level 3 276 to 325	Level 4 326 to 375	Level 5 376 or higher	Overall Proficiency
	n	WGT N (/1,000)	RPCT (SE)	RPCT (SE)	RPCT (SE)	RPCT (SE)	RPCT (SE)	PROF (SE)
Education Level 1								
Still in high school	973	8,268	15 (1.5)	35 (2.3)	38 (2.6)	12 (1.5)	1 (0.6)	274 (1.9)
0 to 8 years	2,167	18,356	79 (1.7)	18 (1.6)	3 (0.8)	0[†](0.1)	0[†](0.0)	170 (2.4)
9 to 12 years	3,311	24,982	46 (1.7)	37 (1.6)	15 (1.3)	2 (0.4)	0[†](0.1)	227 (1.6)
GED	1,062	7,224	17 (2.0)	42 (2.7)	34 (2.3)	7 (1.1)	0[†](0.5)	264 (2.2)
High school	6,107	51,290	20 (0.8)	38 (1.0)	33 (1.1)	9 (0.6)	1 (0.2)	264 (1.1)
Some college (no degree)	6,587	39,634	9 (0.4)	27 (0.8)	42 (1.0)	20 (0.8)	2 (0.4)	290 (0.9)
2 year college degree	1,033	6,831	6 (1.4)	23 (2.0)	43 (2.6)	25 (2.7)	3 (0.9)	299 (2.6)
4 year college degree	2,534	17,804	4 (0.5)	15 (1.3)	37 (1.5)	36 (1.2)	8 (1.2)	314 (1.4)
Graduate studies/degree	2,253	16,306	3 (0.6)	10 (0.9)	34 (1.8)	41 (1.9)	12 (1.1)	326 (1.8)
Education Level 2								
Still in high school	973	8,268	15 (1.5)	35 (2.3)	38 (2.6)	12 (1.5)	1 (0.6)	274 (1.9)
0 to 8 years	2,167	18,356	79 (1.7)	18 (1.6)	3 (0.8)	0[†](0.1)	0[†](0.0)	170 (2.4)
9 to 12 years	3,311	24,982	46 (1.7)	37 (1.6)	15 (1.3)	2 (0.4)	0[†](0.1)	227 (1.6)
GED/high school diploma	7,169	58,514	19 (0.8)	38 (0.9)	33 (1.0)	9 (0.5)	0[†](0.2)	264 (1.0)
Some college (no degree)	6,587	39,634	9 (0.4)	27 (0.8)	42 (1.0)	20 (0.8)	2 (0.4)	290 (0.9)
College degree (2 or more years)	5,820	40,941	4 (0.5)	14 (0.8)	37 (0.8)	36 (1.2)	9 (0.8)	316 (0.9)
Age 1								
16 to 18 years	1,237	10,424	15 (1.4)	34 (2.2)	38 (2.6)	12 (1.9)	1 (0.5)	274 (1.8)
19 to 24 years	3,344	24,515	14 (1.0)	29 (1.4)	37 (1.6)	18 (1.1)	2 (0.4)	280 (1.3)
25 to 39 years	10,050	63,278	16 (0.6)	25 (0.7)	35 (0.6)	21 (0.8)	4 (0.4)	282 (1.0)
40 to 54 years	6,310	43,794	17 (0.8)	27 (0.9)	33 (1.0)	19 (1.0)	3 (0.5)	278 (1.3)
55 to 64 years	2,924	19,503	30 (1.4)	34 (1.4)	26 (1.3)	8 (0.8)	1 (0.3)	249 (1.9)
65 years and older	2,214	29,735	53 (1.5)	32 (1.2)	13 (1.0)	2 (0.5)	0[†](0.1)	217 (2.1)
Age 2								
16 to 24 years	4,581	34,939	14 (0.7)	30 (1.2)	37 (1.5)	16 (1.1)	2 (0.3)	278 (1.1)
25 to 34 years	6,701	41,326	16 (0.7)	25 (0.7)	35 (0.8)	21 (0.9)	4 (0.3)	281 (1.2)
35 to 44 years	5,930	39,755	15 (0.9)	24 (1.0)	35 (1.1)	22 (1.1)	5 (0.5)	283 (1.4)
45 to 54 years	3,729	25,992	18 (1.1)	29 (0.9)	33 (1.4)	17 (0.8)	3 (0.6)	273 (1.4)
55 to 64 years	2,924	19,503	30 (1.4)	34 (1.4)	26 (1.3)	8 (0.8)	1 (0.3)	249 (1.9)
65 years and older	2,214	29,735	53 (1.5)	32 (1.2)	13 (1.0)	2 (0.5)	0[†](0.1)	217 (2.1)

n = sample size; WGT N = population size estimate / 1,000 (the sample sizes for subpopulations may not add up to the total sample sizes, due to missing data); RPCT = row percentage estimate; PROF = average proficiency estimate; (SE) = standard error of the estimate (the reported sample estimate can be said to be within 2 standard errors of the true population value with 95% confidence).

† Percentages less than 0.5 are rounded to zero.

Source: U.S. Department of Education, National Center for Education Statistics, National Adult Literacy Survey, 1992.

TABLE 1.2C

Average Quantitative Proficiency and Literacy Levels by Education Level and Age

EDUCATION LEVEL AND AGE SUBPOPULATIONS	QUANTITATIVE SCALE		Level 1 225 or lower	Level 2 226 to 275	Level 3 276 to 325	Level 4 326 to 375	Level 5 376 or higher	Overall Proficiency
	n	WGT N (/1,000)	RPCT (SE)	RPCT (SE)	RPCT (SE)	RPCT (SE)	RPCT (SE)	PROF (SE)
Education Level 1								
Still in high school	973	8,268	19 (1.7)	35 (3.0)	32 (2.3)	12 (2.0)	1 (0.9)	269 (2.2)
0 to 8 years	2,167	18,356	76 (2.0)	18 (1.8)	5 (1.1)	1 (0.3)	0† (0.2)	169 (3.1)
9 to 12 years	3,311	24,982	45 (1.6)	34 (1.6)	17 (1.3)	3 (0.6)	0† (0.1)	227 (1.7)
GED	1,062	7,224	16 (2.0)	38 (2.5)	35 (2.5)	10 (1.4)	1 (0.5)	268 (2.7)
High school	6,107	51,290	18 (0.8)	33 (1.1)	37 (1.1)	12 (0.5)	1 (0.2)	270 (1.1)
Some college (no degree)	6,587	39,634	8 (0.6)	23 (1.2)	42 (1.4)	23 (1.3)	4 (0.4)	295 (1.4)
2 year college degree	1,033	6,831	4 (0.8)	19 (2.0)	43 (2.0)	29 (2.7)	5 (1.3)	307 (2.8)
4 year college degree	2,534	17,804	4 (0.5)	12 (1.0)	35 (1.4)	38 (1.4)	12 (1.1)	322 (1.2)
Graduate studies/degree	2,253	16,306	2 (0.5)	9 (0.8)	30 (1.4)	42 (1.7)	17 (1.4)	334 (1.3)
Education Level 2								
Still in high school	973	8,268	19 (1.7)	35 (3.0)	32 (2.3)	12 (2.0)	1 (0.9)	269 (2.2)
0 to 8 years	2,167	18,356	76 (2.0)	18 (1.8)	5 (1.1)	1 (0.3)	0† (0.2)	169 (3.1)
9 to 12 years	3,311	24,982	45 (1.6)	34 (1.6)	17 (1.3)	3 (0.6)	0† (0.1)	227 (1.7)
GED/high school diploma	7,169	58,514	18 (0.7)	34 (1.1)	36 (1.0)	11 (0.5)	1 (0.2)	270 (1.0)
Some college (no degree)	6,587	39,634	8 (0.6)	23 (1.2)	42 (1.4)	23 (1.3)	4 (0.4)	295 (1.4)
College degree (2 or more years)	5,820	40,941	3 (0.3)	12 (0.6)	34 (1.0)	38 (1.0)	13 (0.7)	324 (1.0)
Age 1								
16 to 18 years	1,237	10,424	20 (1.7)	35 (2.6)	33 (1.9)	12 (1.5)	1 (0.5)	268 (1.8)
19 to 24 years	3,344	24,515	16 (1.1)	28 (1.4)	37 (1.4)	16 (1.0)	2 (0.5)	277 (1.6)
25 to 39 years	10,050	63,278	17 (0.6)	23 (0.7)	33 (0.6)	21 (0.6)	5 (0.4)	283 (0.9)
40 to 54 years	6,310	43,794	16 (0.9)	22 (1.0)	33 (1.1)	23 (1.1)	6 (0.4)	286 (1.2)
55 to 64 years	2,924	19,503	25 (1.5)	30 (1.9)	30 (1.6)	13 (1.2)	2 (0.6)	261 (2.0)
65 years and older	2,214	29,735	45 (1.6)	26 (1.2)	20 (1.2)	7 (0.7)	2 (0.4)	227 (2.6)
Age 2								
16 to 24 years	4,581	34,939	17 (0.9)	30 (1.1)	36 (1.0)	15 (0.9)	2 (0.4)	274 (1.1)
25 to 34 years	6,701	41,326	17 (0.7)	24 (0.7)	34 (0.8)	20 (0.8)	5 (0.5)	281 (1.1)
35 to 44 years	5,930	39,755	15 (0.8)	21 (1.1)	33 (1.0)	25 (0.7)	6 (0.5)	288 (1.4)
45 to 54 years	3,729	25,992	17 (1.1)	24 (1.2)	33 (1.2)	21 (1.4)	5 (0.5)	282 (1.6)
55 to 64 years	2,924	19,503	25 (1.5)	30 (1.9)	30 (1.6)	13 (1.2)	2 (0.6)	261 (2.0)
65 years and older	2,214	29,735	45 (1.6)	26 (1.2)	20 (1.2)	7 (0.7)	2 (0.4)	227 (2.6)

n = sample size; WGT N = population size estimate / 1,000 (the sample sizes for subpopulations may not add up to the total sample sizes, due to missing data); RPCT = row percentage estimate; PROF = average proficiency estimate; (SE) = standard error of the estimate (the reported sample estimate can be said to be within 2 standard errors of the true population value with 95% confidence).

† Percentages less than 0.5 are rounded to zero.

Source: U.S. Department of Education, National Center for Education Statistics, National Adult Literacy Survey, 1992.

TABLE 1.3A

Characteristics of Respondents by Prose Literacy Levels

DEMOGRAPHIC SUBPOPULATIONS	PROSE SCALE		Level 1 225 or lower	Level 2 226 to 275	Level 3 276 to 325	Level 4 326 to 375	Level 5 376 or higher	Overall Proficiency
	n	WGT N (/1,000)	CPCT (SE)	CPCT (SE)	CPCT (SE)	CPCT (SE)	CPCT (SE)	PROF (SE)
Country of Birth								
Born in the USA	23,376	172,162	75 (0.6)	92 (0.6)	95 (0.6)	96 (0.4)	97 (1.0)	279 (0.7)
Born in another country or territory	2,715	19,127	25 (1.3)	8 (0.9)	5 (1.0)	4 (0.7)	3 (1.0)	212 (2.4)
Education Level 1								
Still in high school	973	8,268	3 (1.5)	6 (1.9)	5 (2.0)	3 (1.4)	1 (0.6)	271 (2.0)
0 to 8 years	2,167	18,356	35 (1.6)	7 (1.3)	1 (0.7)	0† (0.3)	0† (0.0)	177 (2.6)
9 to 12 years	3,311	24,982	27 (1.3)	19 (1.0)	7 (1.0)	2 (0.4)	0† (0.3)	231 (1.5)
GED	1,062	7,224	3 (1.4)	6 (1.8)	5 (2.4)	2 (1.1)	1 (0.7)	268 (1.8)
High school	6,107	51,290	21 (0.8)	36 (1.3)	31 (1.2)	16 (1.0)	4 (1.0)	270 (1.1)
Some college (no degree)	6,587	39,634	8 (0.5)	18 (0.8)	29 (0.9)	26 (0.8)	17 (0.9)	294 (1.0)
2 year college degree	1,033	6,831	1 (0.8)	3 (1.8)	5 (2.2)	7 (2.4)	4 (0.9)	308 (2.4)
4 year college degree	2,534	17,804	2 (0.6)	4 (1.1)	10 (1.2)	22 (1.3)	30 (2.5)	322 (1.6)
Graduate studies/degree	2,253	16,306	1 (0.4)	2 (0.8)	8 (1.2)	23 (1.3)	43 (3.0)	336 (1.4)
Race/Ethnicity								
Black	4,963	21,192	20 (1.0)	15 (1.2)	7 (0.8)	2 (0.4)	1 (0.4)	237 (1.4)
Hispanic	3,126	18,481	23 (1.4)	9 (1.3)	6 (1.1)	3 (0.6)	2 (0.8)	215 (2.2)
Asian/Pacific Islander	438	4,116	4 (3.9)	2 (2.6)	2 (2.7)	1 (1.6)	1 (0.6)	242 (6.7)
American Indian/ Alaskan Native	189	1,803	1 (4.5)!	1 (3.7)!	1 (4.1)!	0† (1.9)!	0† (0.9)!	254 (4.1)!
White	17,292	144,968	51 (0.6)	72 (0.9)	84 (0.7)	92 (0.6)	96 (1.4)	286 (0.7)
Other	83	729	1 (8.9)	0† (5.6)	0† (9.1)	0† (3.7)	0† (0.2)	213 (17.5)
Age 2								
16 to 24 years	4,581	34,939	13 (0.8)	21 (1.3)	21 (1.1)	17 (1.1)	10 (0.9)	278 (1.0)
25 to 34 years	6,701	41,326	16 (0.7)	20 (1.0)	23 (0.8)	26 (1.0)	27 (1.5)	282 (1.2)
35 to 44 years	5,930	39,755	14 (0.6)	16 (0.9)	23 (0.9)	29 (0.9)	36 (1.3)	289 (1.3)
45 to 54 years	3,729	25,992	11 (0.8)	13 (1.1)	14 (1.3)	16 (0.9)	19 (1.0)	282 (1.7)
55 to 64 years	2,924	19,503	13 (1.4)	12 (1.2)	10 (1.1)	7 (0.9)	4 (0.7)	260 (1.9)
65 years and older	2,214	29,735	33 (1.5)	18 (1.5)	9 (1.1)	4 (0.8)	4 (1.1)	230 (2.1)
Any Physical, Mental, Health Condition								
Yes	2,006	22,205	26 (1.0)	13 (1.2)	7 (1.1)	3 (0.7)	2 (0.8)	227 (1.6)
No	23,256	168,879	74 (0.5)	87 (0.7)	93 (0.7)	97 (0.6)	98 (0.8)	278 (0.6)
Visual Difficulty								
Yes	1,801	14,296	19 (1.5)	7 (1.3)	3 (1.1)	2 (1.1)	1 (0.5)	217 (2.4)
No	24,260	176,764	81 (0.4)	93 (0.6)	97 (0.5)	98 (0.5)	99 (0.5)	277 (0.6)
Hearing Difficulty								
Yes	1,611	14,202	13 (1.6)	8 (1.6)	6 (1.2)	4 (0.9)	2 (0.8)	243 (2.6)
No	24,417	176,618	87 (0.4)	92 (0.7)	94 (0.6)	96 (0.6)	98 (0.8)	275 (0.6)
Learning Disability								
Yes	875	5,820	9 (2.1)	2 (2.0)	1 (1.4)	1 (1.1)	1 (0.6)	207 (3.7)
No	25,171	185,190	91 (0.4)	98 (0.6)	99 (0.5)	99 (0.4)	99 (0.4)	275 (0.5)

n = sample size; WGT N = population size estimate / 1,000 (the sample sizes for subpopulations may not add up to the total sample sizes, due to missing data); CPCT = column percentage estimate; PROF = average proficiency estimate; (SE) = standard error of the estimate (the reported sample estimate can be said to be within 2 standard errors of the true population value with 95% confidence).

† Percentages less than 0.5 are rounded to zero.
! Interpret with caution -- the nature of the sample does not allow accurate determination of the variability of this statistic.

Source: U.S. Department of Education, National Center for Education Statistics, National Adult Literacy Survey, 1992.

356-371 0 - 93 - 6 : QL 3

TABLE 1.3B

Characteristics of Respondents by Document Literacy Levels

DEMOGRAPHIC SUBPOPULATIONS	DOCUMENT SCALE		Level 1 225 or lower	Level 2 226 to 275	Level 3 276 to 325	Level 4 326 to 375	Level 5 376 or higher	Overall Proficiency
	n	WGT N (/1,000)	CPCT (SE)	CPCT (SE)	CPCT (SE)	CPCT (SE)	CPCT (SE)	PROF (SE)
Country of Birth								
Born in the USA	23,376	172,162	78 (0.5)	92 (0.4)	94 (0.5)	96 (0.5)	97 (0.4)	273 (0.7)
Born in another country or territory	2,715	19,127	22 (1.3)	8 (1.0)	6 (1.0)	4 (0.7)	3 (0.4)	212 (2.3)
Education Level 1								
Still in high school	973	8,268	3 (1.3)	5 (2.0)	5 (2.0)	3 (1.2)	2 (0.9)	274 (1.9)
0 to 8 years	2,167	18,356	33 (1.5)	6 (1.5)	1 (0.6)	0[†](0.1)	0[†](0.0)	170 (2.4)
9 to 12 years	3,311	24,982	26 (1.5)	17 (1.3)	6 (1.1)	2 (0.4)	1 (0.3)	227 (1.6)
GED	1,062	7,224	3 (1.7)	6 (1.9)	4 (2.1)	2 (0.9)	1 (0.7)	264 (2.2)
High school	6,107	51,290	23 (0.8)	36 (0.9)	29 (0.9)	15 (0.7)	5 (1.5)	264 (1.1)
Some college (no degree)	6,587	39,634	8 (0.5)	20 (0.8)	28 (0.9)	27 (0.9)	20 (1.7)	290 (0.9)
2 year college degree	1,033	6,831	1 (1.3)	3 (1.7)	5 (2.1)	6 (2.1)	5 (1.0)	299 (2.6)
4 year college degree	2,534	17,804	2 (0.4)	5 (1.1)	11 (1.2)	22 (1.0)	28 (2.8)	314 (1.4)
Graduate studies/degree	2,253	16,306	1 (0.4)	3 (0.7)	9 (1.1)	23 (1.4)	39 (3.7)	326 (1.8)
Race/Ethnicity								
Black	4,963	21,192	20 (0.9)	14 (1.0)	6 (0.8)	2 (0.3)	1 (0.2)	230 (1.2)
Hispanic	3,126	18,481	21 (1.7)	9 (1.3)	6 (1.1)	3 (0.7)	2 (0.9)	213 (2.5)
Asian/Pacific Islander	438	4,116	3 (3.2)	2 (2.4)	2 (2.8)	2 (2.0)	1 (0.8)	245 (5.6)
American Indian/ Alaskan Native	189	1,803	1 (4.0)!	1 (4.2)!	1 (5.1)!	0[†](3.0)!	0[†](0.3)!	254 (4.9)!
White	17,292	144,968	54 (0.7)	73 (0.7)	85 (0.7)	92 (0.5)	95 (0.9)	280 (0.8)
Other	83	729	1 (9.7)	0[†](5.8)	0[†](5.5)	0[†](4.1)	0[†](0.4)	213 (15.5)
Age 2								
16 to 24 years	4,581	34,939	11 (0.6)	20 (1.0)	22 (1.0)	19 (1.3)	14 (0.9)	278 (1.1)
25 to 34 years	6,701	41,326	15 (0.7)	19 (0.7)	24 (0.7)	29 (1.0)	30 (1.6)	281 (1.2)
35 to 44 years	5,930	39,755	14 (0.8)	18 (1.0)	23 (1.1)	29 (1.1)	36 (1.6)	283 (1.4)
45 to 54 years	3,729	25,992	11 (1.0)	14 (0.8)	14 (1.0)	15 (0.7)	15 (2.3)	273 (1.4)
55 to 64 years	2,924	19,503	13 (1.3)	12 (1.1)	9 (1.1)	5 (0.7)	4 (0.9)	249 (1.9)
65 years and older	2,214	29,735	35 (1.5)	17 (1.2)	7 (0.9)	2 (0.5)	2 (0.6)	217 (2.1)
Any Physical, Mental, Health Condition								
Yes	2,806	22,205	26 (1.2)	12 (1.1)	6 (0.7)	3 (0.6)	2 (0.8)	219 (1.9)
No	23,256	168,879	74 (0.5)	88 (0.5)	94 (0.5)	97 (0.4)	98 (0.8)	273 (0.6)
Visual Difficulty								
Yes	1,801	14,296	18 (1.3)	7 (1.3)	3 (1.1)	2 (0.7)	2 (0.5)	212 (2.6)
No	24,260	176,764	82 (0.5)	93 (0.6)	97 (0.6)	98 (0.4)	98 (0.5)	271 (0.6)
Hearing Difficulty								
Yes	1,611	14,202	13 (2.0)	8 (1.7)	5 (1.2)	4 (0.8)	2 (0.7)	236 (2.8)
No	24,417	176,618	87 (0.5)	92 (0.5)	95 (0.5)	96 (0.5)	98 (0.7)	269 (0.6)
Learning Disability								
Yes	875	5,820	8 (2.3)	2 (2.2)	1 (1.1)	1 (0.8)	2 (1.0)	201 (4.0)
No	25,171	185,190	92 (0.4)	98 (0.5)	99 (0.4)	99 (0.4)	98 (0.7)	269 (0.7)

n = sample size; WGT N = population size estimate / 1,000 (the sample sizes for subpopulations may not add up to the total sample sizes, due to missing data); CPCT = column percentage estimate; PROF = average proficiency estimate; (SE) = standard error of the estimate (the reported sample estimate can be said to be within 2 standard errors of the true population value with 95% confidence).

[†] Percentages less than 0.5 are rounded to zero.

! Interpret with caution -- the nature of the sample does not allow accurate determination of the variability of this statistic.

Source: U.S. Department of Education, National Center for Education Statistics, National Adult Literacy Survey, 1992.

TABLE 1.3C

Characteristics of Respondents by Quantitative Literacy Levels

DEMOGRAPHIC SUBPOPULATIONS	QUANTITATIVE SCALE		Level 1 225 or lower	Level 2 226 to 275	Level 3 276 to 325	Level 4 326 to 375	Level 5 376 or higher	Overall Proficiency
	n	WGT N (/1,000)	CPCT (SE)	CPCT (SE)	CPCT (SE)	CPCT (SE)	CPCT (SE)	PROF (SE)
Country of Birth								
Born in the USA	23,376	172,162	78 (0.5)	91 (0.6)	94 (0.5)	95 (0.4)	96 (1.1)	278 (0.8)
Born in another country or territory	2,715	19,127	22 (1.2)	9 (1.0)	6 (0.9)	5 (0.6)	4 (1.1)	214 (2.8)
Education Level 1								
Still in high school	973	8,268	4 (1.4)	6 (2.2)	4 (2.0)	3 (1.4)	1 (1.0)	269 (2.2)
0 to 8 years	2,167	18,356	33 (1.6)	7 (1.3)	2 (0.8)	0† (0.2)	1 (0.3)	169 (3.1)
9 to 12 years	3,311	24,982	27 (1.5)	17 (1.3)	7 (1.0)	2 (0.6)	1 (0.2)	227 (1.7)
GED	1,062	7,224	3 (1.6)	6 (2.1)	4 (2.1)	2 (1.2)	1 (0.5)	268 (2.7)
High school	6,107	51,290	22 (0.9)	35 (1.1)	31 (1.1)	18 (0.6)	7 (0.9)	270 (1.1)
Some college (no degree)	6,587	39,634	8 (0.6)	19 (1.1)	28 (1.0)	28 (1.3)	20 (1.2)	295 (1.4)
2 year college degree	1,033	6,831	1 (0.7)	3 (1.6)	5 (1.6)	6 (2.2)	5 (1.2)	307 (2.8)
4 year college degree	2,534	17,804	2 (0.5)	4 (0.8)	10 (1.2)	20 (1.1)	28 (1.5)	322 (1.2)
Graduate studies/degree	2,253	16,306	1 (0.4)	3 (0.7)	8 (1.2)	21 (1.5)	38 (2.1)	334 (1.3)
Race/Ethnicity								
Black	4,963	21,192	23 (0.9)	15 (0.8)	6 (0.8)	2 (0.4)	1 (0.1)	224 (1.4)
Hispanic	3,126	18,481	22 (1.3)	10 (1.1)	6 (1.0)	3 (0.8)	2 (0.4)	212 (2.5)
Asian/Pacific Islander	438	4,116	3 (3.6)	2 (2.9)	2 (2.8)	2 (2.0)	2 (1.5)	256 (6.7)
American Indian/ Alaskan Native	189	1,803	1 (5.0)!	1 (5.4)!	1 (3.4)!	0† (1.4)!	0† (0.8)!	250 (5.1)!
White	17,292	144,968	50 (0.5)	72 (0.6)	85 (0.6)	93 (0.6)	95 (0.8)	287 (0.8)
Other	83	729	1 (7.5)	0† (6.6)	0† (9.1)	0† (2.3)	0† (0.6)	220 (13.1)
Age 2								
16 to 24 years	4,581	34,939	14 (0.8)	22 (0.9)	21 (0.8)	16 (0.9)	9 (1.7)	274 (1.1)
25 to 34 years	6,701	41,326	17 (0.7)	21 (0.7)	23 (0.7)	25 (0.8)	26 (1.6)	281 (1.1)
35 to 44 years	5,930	39,755	14 (0.7)	17 (1.0)	22 (0.8)	29 (0.7)	33 (0.7)	288 (1.4)
45 to 54 years	3,729	25,992	11 (1.0)	13 (0.9)	14 (0.9)	16 (1.3)	19 (1.3)	282 (1.6)
55 to 64 years	2,924	19,503	12 (1.3)	12 (1.2)	10 (1.4)	8 (0.9)	6 (1.0)	261 (2.0)
65 years and older	2,214	29,735	32 (1.5)	16 (1.1)	10 (1.1)	6 (0.7)	7 (0.9)	227 (2.6)
Any Physical, Mental, Health Condition								
Yes	2,806	22,205	26 (1.2)	12 (0.9)	7 (1.0)	4 (0.7)	3 (0.7)	220 (2.4)
No	23,256	168,879	74 (0.5)	88 (0.5)	93 (0.5)	96 (0.3)	97 (0.7)	278 (0.6)
Visual Difficulty								
Yes	1,801	14,296	19 (1.4)	7 (1.3)	4 (1.2)	2 (0.7)	2 (0.6)	210 (2.7)
No	24,260	176,764	81 (0.5)	93 (0.5)	96 (0.5)	98 (0.5)	98 (0.5)	276 (0.7)
Hearing Difficulty								
Yes	1,611	14,202	12 (2.1)	7 (1.7)	6 (1.7)	4 (1.1)	4 (1.0)	242 (3.6)
No	24,417	176,618	88 (0.5)	93 (0.5)	94 (0.5)	96 (0.6)	96 (1.0)	274 (0.7)
Learning Disability								
Yes	875	5,820	8 (2.7)	3 (2.3)	1 (1.3)	1 (1.1)	1 (0.5)	197 (4.2)
No	25,171	185,190	92 (0.4)	97 (0.4)	99 (0.4)	99 (0.3)	99 (0.3)	274 (0.7)

n = sample size; WGT N = population size estimate / 1,000 (the sample sizes for subpopulations may not add up to the total sample sizes, due to missing data); CPCT = column percentage estimate; PROF = average proficiency estimate; (SE) = standard error of the estimate (the reported sample estimate can be said to be within 2 standard errors of the true population value with 95% confidence).

† Percentages less than 0.5 are rounded to zero.
! Interpret with caution -- the nature of the sample does not allow accurate determination of the variability of this statistic.

Source: U.S. Department of Education, National Center for Education Statistics, National Adult Literacy Survey, 1992.

TABLE 1.4A

Average Prose Proficiency and Literacy Levels
Incarcerated Sample by Total, Education Level, and Age

DEMOGRAPHIC SUBPOPULATIONS	PROSE SCALE		Level 1 225 or lower	Level 2 226 to 275	Level 3 276 to 325	Level 4 326 to 375	Level 5 376 or higher	Overall Proficiency
	n	WGT N (/1,000)	RPCT (SE)	RPCT (SE)	RPCT (SE)	RPCT (SE)	RPCT (SE)	PROF (SE)
Total Population								
Total	1,147	766	31 (1.7)	37 (2.0)	26 (1.6)	6 (0.8)	0†(0.2)	246 (1.9)
Education Level								
0 to 8 years	157	107	66 (4.2)	24 (3.8)	10 (4.0)	1 (0.6)	0†(0.0)	196 (5.0)
9 to 12 years	385	271	41 (3.1)	44 (3.5)	14 (2.4)	1 (0.6)	0†(0.0)	230 (3.0)
GED	183	130	10 (3.1)	44 (4.9)	39 (5.6)	6 (3.0)	0†(0.3)	270 (4.3)
High school	154	107	25 (5.3)	39 (5.0)	32 (6.0)	5 (2.0)	0†(0.0)	255 (5.0)
Some college (no degree)	211	120	10 (2.2)	28 (4.2)	42 (4.4)	18 (4.4)	2 (1.4)	285 (4.2)
2 year college degree	27	15	*** (****)	*** (****)	*** (****)	*** (****)	*** (****)	*** (****)
4 year college degree	17	9	*** (****)	*** (****)	*** (****)	*** (****)	*** (****)	*** (****)
Graduate studies/degree	9	5	*** (****)	*** (****)	*** (****)	*** (****)	*** (****)	*** (****)
Age								
16 to 18 years	19	12	*** (****)	*** (****)	*** (****)	*** (****)	*** (****)	*** (****)
19 to 24 years	262	162	27 (3.3)	42 (4.6)	26 (4.1)	6 (2.1)	0†(0.2)	252 (3.6)
25 to 39 years	641	438	32 (2.0)	36 (2.4)	26 (2.5)	5 (0.9)	0†(0.4)	245 (2.5)
40 to 54 years	192	132	32 (4.0)	36 (4.0)	24 (3.3)	8 (2.6)	0†(0.5)	241 (5.8)
55 to 64 years	20	13	*** (****)	*** (****)	*** (****)	*** (****)	*** (****)	*** (****)
65 years and older	10	7	*** (****)	*** (****)	*** (****)	*** (****)	*** (****)	*** (****)

n = sample size; WGT N = population size estimate / 1,000 (the sample sizes for subpopulations may not add up to the total sample sizes, due to missing data); RPCT = row percentage estimate; PROF = average proficiency estimate; (SE) = standard error of the estimate (the reported sample estimate can be said to be within 2 standard errors of the true population value with 95% confidence).

† Percentages less than 0.5 are rounded to zero.
*** Sample size is insufficient to permit a reliable estimate (fewer than 45 respondents).

Source: U.S. Department of Education, National Center for Education Statistics, National Adult Literacy Survey, 1992.

TABLE 1.4B

Average Document Proficiency and Literacy Levels
Incarcerated Sample by Total, Education Level, and Age

DEMOGRAPHIC SUBPOPULATIONS	DOCUMENT SCALE		Level 1 225 or lower	Level 2 226 to 275	Level 3 276 to 325	Level 4 326 to 375	Level 5 376 or higher	Overall Proficiency
	n	WGT N (/1,000)	RPCT (SE)	RPCT (SE)	RPCT (SE)	RPCT (SE)	RPCT (SE)	PROF (SE)
Total Population								
Total	1,147	766	33 (2.1)	38 (2.1)	25 (1.5)	4 (0.9)	0†(0.2)	240 (2.2)
Education Level								
0 to 8 years	157	107	69 (3.6)	23 (4.1)	7 (2.6)	1 (0.5)	0†(0.0)	176 (6.1)
9 to 12 years	385	271	41 (3.0)	43 (3.9)	14 (2.7)	2 (1.0)	0†(0.0)	230 (2.8)
GED	183	130	16 (3.3)	47 (6.2)	32 (5.0)	4 (2.7)	0†(0.3)	263 (4.3)
High school	154	107	27 (4.9)	37 (5.7)	32 (4.7)	4 (2.4)	0†(0.0)	251 (5.6)
Some college (no degree)	211	120	12 (2.5)	30 (3.5)	45 (4.5)	13 (3.4)	1 (1.0)	280 (3.7)
2 year college degree	27	15	*** (****)	*** (****)	*** (****)	*** (****)	*** (****)	*** (****)
4 year college degree	17	9	*** (****)	*** (****)	*** (****)	*** (****)	*** (****)	*** (****)
Graduate studies/degree	9	5	*** (****)	*** (****)	*** (****)	*** (****)	*** (****)	*** (****)
Age								
16 to 18 years	19	12	*** (****)	*** (****)	*** (****)	*** (****)	*** (****)	*** (****)
19 to 24 years	262	162	26 (3.4)	41 (5.0)	27 (4.3)	5 (2.2)	0†(0.2)	251 (3.6)
25 to 39 years	641	438	33 (2.7)	37 (2.7)	25 (2.4)	4 (1.3)	0†(0.2)	240 (3.2)
40 to 54 years	192	132	38 (5.3)	37 (4.5)	19 (3.1)	6 (1.9)	0†(0.4)	230 (6.3)
55 to 64 years	20	13	*** (****)	*** (****)	*** (****)	*** (****)	*** (****)	*** (****)
65 years and older	10	7	*** (****)	*** (****)	*** (****)	*** (****)	*** (****)	*** (****)

n = sample size; WGT N = population size estimate / 1,000 (the sample sizes for subpopulations may not add up to the total sample sizes, due to missing data); RPCT = row percentage estimate; PROF = average proficiency estimate; (SE) = standard error of the estimate (the reported sample estimate can be said to be within 2 standard errors of the true population value with 95% confidence).

† Percentages less than 0.5 are rounded to zero.
*** Sample size is insufficient to permit a reliable estimate (fewer than 45 respondents).

Source: U.S. Department of Education, National Center for Education Statistics, National Adult Literacy Survey, 1992.

TABLE 1.4C

Average Quantitative Proficiency and Literacy Levels
Incarcerated Sample by Total, Education Level, and Age

DEMOGRAPHIC SUBPOPULATIONS	QUANTITATIVE SCALE		Level 1 225 or lower	Level 2 226 to 275	Level 3 276 to 325	Level 4 326 to 375	Level 5 376 or higher	Overall Proficiency
	n	WGT N (/1,000)	RPCT (SE)	RPCT (SE)	RPCT (SE)	RPCT (SE)	RPCT (SE)	PROF (SE)
Total								
Total	1,147	766	40 (1.9)	32 (2.2)	22 (1.9)	6 (1.0)	1 (0.4)	236 (3.1)
Education Level								
0 to 8 years	157	107	70 (5.1)	21 (3.5)	7 (2.6)	2 (1.4)	0†(0.4)	182 (8.4)
9 to 12 years	385	271	51 (2.8)	34 (3.4)	13 (2.1)	2 (0.9)	0†(0.3)	219 (3.5)
GED	183	130	21 (5.2)	40 (5.6)	32 (5.7)	7 (2.5)	0†(1.4)	263 (4.6)
High school	154	107	36 (5.0)	32 (5.8)	26 (4.3)	6 (3.0)	0†(0.3)	244 (6.7)
Some college (no degree)	211	120	15 (3.0)	31 (4.7)	36 (4.8)	15 (3.5)	3 (1.2)	276 (3.6)
2 year college degree	27	15	*** (****)	*** (****)	*** (****)	*** (****)	*** (****)	*** (****)
4 year college degree	17	9	*** (****)	*** (****)	*** (****)	*** (****)	*** (****)	*** (****)
Graduate studies/degree	9	5	*** (****)	*** (****)	*** (****)	*** (****)	*** (****)	*** (****)
Age								
16 to 18 years	19	12	*** (****)	*** (****)	*** (****)	*** (****)	*** (****)	*** (****)
19 to 24 years	262	162	39 (3.8)	33 (3.4)	22 (4.5)	5 (1.5)	1 (1.3)	241 (4.4)
25 to 39 years	641	438	40 (2.0)	32 (2.5)	22 (2.4)	6 (1.3)	1 (0.4)	236 (3.5)
40 to 54 years	192	132	40 (4.6)	30 (4.5)	23 (3.4)	6 (1.6)	1 (0.9)	232 (7.3)
55 to 64 years	20	13	*** (****)	*** (****)	*** (****)	*** (****)	*** (****)	*** (****)
65 years and older	10	7	*** (****)	*** (****)	*** (****)	*** (****)	*** (****)	*** (****)

n = sample size; WGT N = population size estimate / 1,000 (the sample sizes for subpopulations may not add up to the total sample sizes, due to missing data); RPCT = row percentage estimate; PROF = average proficiency estimate; (SE) = standard error of the estimate (the reported sample estimate can be said to be within 2 standard errors of the true population value with 95% confidence).

† Percentages less than 0.5 are rounded to zero.
*** Sample size is insufficient to permit a reliable estimate (fewer than 45 respondents).

Source: U.S. Department of Education, National Center for Education Statistics, National Adult Literacy Survey, 1992.

TABLE 1.5

Average Proficiency on Each Literacy Scale for the 1985 YALS and 1992 NALS Populations

TOTAL AND RACE/ETHNICITY BY RESPONDENTS' AGE	AVERAGE PROFICIENCY		Prose	Document	Quantitative
	n	WGT N (/1,000)	CPCT (SE) PROF (SE)	CPCT (SE) PROF (SE)	CPCT (SE) PROF (SE)
1985 Age 21-25					
Total Population	3,618	21,158	100 (0.0) 293 (2.3)	100 (0.0) 292 (2.2)	100 (0.0) 293 (2.0)
White	2,016	16,115	76 (1.6) 305 (1.9)	76 (1.6) 305 (1.9)	76 (1.6) 304 (1.8)
Black	991	2,801	13 (1.1) 248 (2.6)!	13 (1.1) 248 (2.6)!	13 (1.1) 252 (2.5)!
Hispanic	478	1,481	7 (1.0) 251 (8.1)!	7 (1.0) 243 (9.4)!	7 (1.0) 253 (8.9)!
Other	133	761	4 (0.6) 289 (8.0)!	4 (0.6) 285 (6.1)!	4 (0.6) 286 (7.2)!
1992 Age 21-25					
Total Population	2,690	20,300	100 (0.0) 281 (1.7)	100 (0.0) 281 (1.7)	100 (0.0) 279 (1.8)
White	1,654	14,252	70 (1.2) 296 (2.1)	70 (1.2) 296 (1.9)	70 (1.2) 295 (2.3)
Black	494	2,226	11 (0.7) 256 (2.5)!	11 (0.7) 254 (3.2)!	11 (0.7) 244 (3.1)!
Hispanic	445	2,974	15 (1.0) 231 (5.3)	15 (1.0) 233 (5.7)	15 (1.0) 229 (5.5)
Other	97	848	4 (0.7) 278 (6.5)!	4 (0.7) 277 (6.2)!	4 (0.7) 278 (6.9)!
1992 Age 28-32					
Total Population	3,265	21,215	100 (0.0) 283 (1.9)	100 (0.0) 281 (1.8)	100 (0.0) 282 (1.7)
White	2,069	15,017	71 (1.2) 301 (1.7)	71 (1.2) 300 (1.5)	71 (1.2) 301 (1.6)
Black	628	2,609	12 (0.5) 251 (2.5)	12 (0.5) 245 (2.5)	12 (0.5) 240 (2.5)
Hispanic	468	2,749	13 (0.7) 223 (5.2)	13 (0.7) 225 (4.9)	13 (0.7) 223 (5.1)
Other	100	838	4 (0.7) 253 (11.0)!	4 (0.7) 257 (9.1)!	4 (0.7) 264 (7.9)!

n = sample size; WGT N = population size estimate / 1,000 (the sample sizes for subpopulations may not add up to the total sample sizes, due to missing data); CPCT = column percentage estimate; PROF = average proficiency estimate; (SE) = standard error of the estimate (the reported sample estimate can be said to be within 2 standard errors of the true population value with 95% confidence).

! Interpret with caution -- the nature of the sample does not allow accurate determination of the variability of this statistic.

Source: U.S. Department of Education, National Center for Education Statistics, National Adult Literacy Survey, 1992.

TABLE 1.6

Average Proficiency on Each Literacy Scale
Respondents' Education Level by Parents' Education Level

RESPONDENTS' EDUCATION LEVEL	PARENTS' EDUCATION LEVEL		0 to 8 years	9 to 12 years	High school	4 years college (degree)
	n	WGT N (/1,000)	RPCT (SE) PROF (SE)	RPCT (SE) PROF (SE)	RPCT (SE) PROF (SE)	RPCT (SE) PROF (SE)
0 to 8 years	1,412	11,983				
Prose			77 (1.6) 174 (2.8)	8 (1.0) 191 (7.4)!	13 (1.4) 208 (7.7)!	2 (0.5) *** (****)
Document			77 (1.6) 166 (2.9)	8 (1.0) 182 (7.4)!	13 (1.4) 202 (7.0)!	2 (0.5) *** (****)
Quantitative			77 (1.6) 169 (3.8)	8 (1.0) 181 (7.8)!	13 (1.4) 200 (8.5)!	2 (0.5) *** (****)
9 to 12 years	2,245	16,932				
Prose			46 (1.4) 218 (2.1)	19 (1.1) 235 (3.5)	30 (1.5) 244 (2.7)	5 (0.7) 255 (7.1)!
Document			46 (1.4) 211 (2.3)	19 (1.1) 232 (4.3)	30 (1.5) 243 (2.8)	5 (0.7) 257 (7.0)!
Quantitative			46 (1.4) 217 (2.8)	19 (1.1) 232 (4.6)	30 (1.5) 242 (3.2)	5 (0.7) 256 (6.6)!
High school	4,577	37,485				
Prose			28 (1.0) 255 (2.5)	15 (0.7) 267 (3.1)	48 (1.0) 275 (1.7)	9 (0.6) 286 (3.5)
Document			28 (1.0) 245 (2.5)	15 (0.7) 260 (2.3)	48 (1.0) 271 (1.6)	9 (0.6) 286 (4.4)
Quantitative			28 (1.0) 255 (2.5)	15 (0.7) 266 (3.4)	48 (1.0) 277 (1.8)	9 (0.6) 284 (3.5)
4 year college degree	1,487	10,683				
Prose			14 (1.1) 296 (4.1)!	7 (0.9) 308 (5.9)!	43 (2.0) 318 (2.2)	35 (1.7) 324 (2.3)
Document			14 (1.1) 284 (4.0)!	7 (0.9) 294 (6.9)!	43 (2.0) 310 (2.2)	35 (1.7) 320 (2.4)
Quantitative			14 (1.1) 303 (4.8)!	7 (0.9) 313 (7.1)!	43 (2.0) 320 (2.2)	35 (1.7) 324 (2.4)
Total Population	17,266	126,380				
Prose			31 (0.6) 233 (1.5)	13 (0.4) 264 (1.7)	41 (0.6) 284 (0.9)	16 (0.4) 305 (1.4)
Document			31 (0.6) 225 (1.6)	13 (0.4) 258 (1.7)	41 (0.6) 279 (0.7)	16 (0.4) 302 (1.5)
Quantitative			31 (0.6) 233 (1.7)	13 (0.4) 264 (2.0)	41 (0.6) 284 (0.9)	16 (0.4) 304 (1.9)

n = sample size; WGT N = population size estimate / 1,000 (the sample sizes for subpopulations may not add up to the total sample sizes, due to missing data); RPCT = row percentage estimate; PROF = average proficiency estimate; (SE) = standard error of the estimate (the reported sample estimate can be said to be within 2 standard errors of the true population value with 95% confidence).

*** Sample size is insufficient to permit a reliable estimate (fewer than 45 respondents).
! Interpret with caution -- the nature of the sample does not allow accurate determination of the variability of this statistic.

Source: U.S. Department of Education, National Center for Education Statistics, National Adult Literacy Survey, 1992.

TABLE 1.7

Average Proficiency on Each Literacy Scale
Education Level by Race/Ethnicity

EDUCATION LEVEL	RACE/ETHNICITY n WGT N (/1,000)	Black RPCT (SE) PROF (SE)	Hispanic RPCT (SE) PROF (SE)	Asian/ Pacific Islander RPCT (SE) PROF (SE)	American Indian/ Alaskan Native RPCT (SE) PROF (SE)	White RPCT (SE) PROF (SE)	Other RPCT (SE) PROF (SE)
Still in high school	973 8,268						
Prose		16 (1.5) 247 (3.9)	13 (1.1) 246 (6.7)!	2 (0.7) *** (****)	1 (0.8) *** (****)	67 (1.9) 283 (2.2)	1 (0.5) *** (****)
Document		16 (1.5) 248 (3.9)	13 (1.1) 246 (6.1)!	2 (0.7) *** (****)	1 (0.8) *** (****)	67 (1.9) 286 (2.3)	1 (0.5) *** (****)
Quantitative		16 (1.5) 234 (4.7)	13 (1.1) 241 (6.5)!	2 (0.7) *** (****)	1 (0.8) *** (****)	67 (1.9) 283 (2.4)	1 (0.5) *** (****)
0 to 8 years	2,167 18,356						
Prose		13 (0.8) 159 (3.9)	25 (0.9) 135 (3.6)	2 (0.8) *** (****)	1 (0.3) *** (****)	57 (1.5) 202 (3.1)	1 (0.3) *** (****)
Document		13 (0.8) 151 (2.8)	25 (0.9) 131 (3.6)	2 (0.8) *** (****)	1 (0.3) *** (****)	57 (1.5) 191 (3.1)	1 (0.3) *** (****)
Quantitative		13 (0.8) 140 (4.0)	25 (0.9) 128 (3.7)	2 (0.8) *** (****)	1 (0.3) *** (****)	57 (1.5) 195 (3.8)	1 (0.3) *** (****)
9 to 12 years	3,311 24,982						
Prose		18 (0.6) 213 (2.3)	13 (0.7) 200 (4.8)	1 (0.3) *** (****)	1 (0.4) *** (****)	66 (1.1) 243 (1.6)	0[†] (0.1) *** (****)
Document		18 (0.6) 207 (2.2)	13 (0.7) 197 (4.9)	1 (0.3) *** (****)	1 (0.4) *** (****)	66 (1.1) 238 (1.9)	0[†] (0.1) *** (****)
Quantitative		18 (0.6) 197 (2.9)	13 (0.7) 196 (5.4)	1 (0.3) *** (****)	1 (0.4) *** (****)	66 (1.1) 242 (2.1)	0[†] (0.1) *** (****)
GED	1,062 7,224						
Prose		10 (1.1) 243 (4.1)!	12 (1.3) 240 (6.8)!	1 (0.3) *** (****)	3 (1.1) *** (****)	74 (2.1) 276 (2.0)	1 (0.4) *** (****)
Document		10 (1.1) 235 (4.2)!	12 (1.3) 236 (6.4)!	1 (0.3) *** (****)	3 (1.1) *** (****)	74 (2.1) 272 (2.2)	1 (0.4) *** (****)
Quantitative		10 (1.1) 235 (4.5)!	12 (1.3) 240 (7.8)!	1 (0.3) *** (****)	3 (1.1) *** (****)	74 (2.1) 277 (3.1)	1 (0.4) *** (****)
High school diploma	6,107 51,290						
Prose		11 (0.4) 242 (1.6)	7 (0.4) 242 (4.4)	1 (0.2) 209 (16.0)!	1 (0.3) *** (****)	79 (0.8) 278 (1.2)	0[†] (0.1) *** (****)
Document		11 (0.4) 235 (1.7)	7 (0.4) 242 (4.9)	1 (0.2) 214 (13.2)!	1 (0.3) *** (****)	79 (0.8) 271 (1.2)	0[†] (0.1) *** (****)
Quantitative		11 (0.4) 232 (2.0)	7 (0.4) 240 (4.8)	1 (0.2) 227 (12.5)!	1 (0.3) *** (****)	79 (0.8) 279 (1.2)	0[†] (0.1) *** (****)
Some college (no degree)	6,587 39,634						
Prose		10 (0.5) 267 (1.9)	8 (0.3) 265 (3.5)	2 (0.2) 264 (8.3)!	1 (0.4) *** (****)	78 (0.8) 302 (1.2)	0[†] (0.1) *** (****)
Document		10 (0.5) 261 (2.2)	8 (0.3) 263 (3.4)	2 (0.2) 261 (10.2)!	1 (0.4) *** (****)	78 (0.8) 297 (1.0)	0[†] (0.1) *** (****)
Quantitative		10 (0.5) 258 (2.2)	8 (0.3) 265 (3.5)	2 (0.2) 273 (7.7)!	1 (0.4) *** (****)	78 (0.8) 304 (1.5)	0[†] (0.1) *** (****)
2 year college degree	1,033 6,831						
Prose		8 (1.1) 276 (4.8)!	6 (0.7) 291 (6.5)!	2 (0.6) *** (****)	1 (0.5) *** (****)	83 (1.3) 313 (2.6)	0[†] (0.1) *** (****)
Document		8 (1.1) 263 (4.8)!	6 (0.7) 288 (6.0)!	2 (0.6) *** (****)	1 (0.5) *** (****)	83 (1.3) 305 (2.8)	0[†] (0.1) *** (****)
Quantitative		8 (1.1) 267 (3.5)!	6 (0.7) 286 (7.6)!	2 (0.6) *** (****)	1 (0.5) *** (****)	83 (1.3) 313 (2.9)	0[†] (0.1) *** (****)
4 year college degree	2,534 17,804						
Prose		6 (0.5) 288 (3.3)!	4 (0.6) 282 (8.2)!	4 (0.6) 271 (8.8)!	0[†] (0.1) *** (****)	85 (0.7) 328 (1.7)	0[†] (0.0) *** (****)
Document		6 (0.5) 279 (4.1)!	4 (0.6) 285 (7.3)!	4 (0.6) 275 (8.6)!	0[†] (0.1) *** (****)	85 (0.7) 320 (1.5)	0[†] (0.0) *** (****)
Quantitative		6 (0.5) 280 (3.1)!	4 (0.6) 286 (8.6)!	4 (0.6) 286 (9.2)!	0[†] (0.1) *** (****)	85 (0.7) 329 (1.4)	0[†] (0.0) *** (****)
Graduate studies/degree	2,253 16,306						
Prose		5 (0.5) 298 (5.2)!	3 (0.5) 312 (9.2)!	4 (0.6) 301 (5.7)!	0[†] (0.1) *** (****)	88 (0.9) 341 (1.4)	0[†] (0.1) *** (****)
Document		5 (0.5) 285 (5.2)!	3 (0.5) 306 (10.3)!	4 (0.6) 298 (6.2)!	0[†] (0.1) *** (****)	88 (0.9) 330 (1.9)	0[†] (0.1) *** (****)
Quantitative		5 (0.5) 285 (4.9)!	3 (0.5) 312 (9.1)!	4 (0.6) 314 (7.4)!	0[†] (0.1) *** (****)	88 (0.9) 338 (1.4)	0[†] (0.1) *** (****)

n = sample size; WGT N = population size estimate / 1,000 (the sample sizes for subpopulations may not add up to the total sample sizes, due to missing data); RPCT = row percentage estimate; PROF = average proficiency estimate; (SE) = standard error of the estimate (the reported sample estimate can be said to be within 2 standard errors of the true population value with 95% confidence).

† Percentages less than 0.5 are rounded to zero.
*** Sample size is insufficient to permit a reliable estimate (fewer than 45 respondents).
! Interpret with caution -- the nature of the sample does not allow accurate determination of the variability of this statistic.

Source: U.S. Department of Education, National Center for Education Statistics, National Adult Literacy Survey, 1992.

TABLE 1.8

Average Proficiency on Each Literacy Scale
Age by Race/Ethnicity

AGE	RACE/ETHNICITY		Black	Hispanic	Asian/Pacific Islander	American Indian/Alaskan Native	White	Other
	n	WGT N (/1,000)	RPCT (SE) PROF (SE)	RPCT (SE) PROF (SE)	RPCT (SE) PROF (SE)	RPCT (SE) PROF (SE)	RPCT (SE) PROF (SE)	RPCT (SE) PROF (SE)
16 to 18 years	1,237	10,424						
Prose			16 (1.3) 248 (3.6)	13 (1.1) 237 (6.7)	2 (0.6) *** (****)	2 (0.7) *** (****)	66 (1.8) 284 (2.0)	1 (0.4) *** (****)
Document			16 (1.3) 248 (3.7)	13 (1.1) 237 (5.7)	2 (0.6) *** (****)	2 (0.7) *** (****)	66 (1.8) 287 (2.2)	1 (0.4) *** (****)
Quantitative			16 (1.3) 236 (4.0)	13 (1.1) 230 (5.9)	2 (0.6) *** (****)	2 (0.7) *** (****)	66 (1.8) 283 (2.0)	1 (0.4) *** (****)
19 to 24 years	3,344	24,515						
Prose			13 (0.6) 254 (1.7)	15 (0.8) 238 (4.9)	3 (0.5) 279 (8.6)!	1 (0.5) *** (****)	68 (1.3) 295 (1.5)	0†(0.2) *** (****)
Document			13 (0.6) 251 (1.9)	15 (0.8) 238 (5.4)	3 (0.5) 278 (8.4)!	1 (0.5) *** (****)	68 (1.3) 295 (1.4)	0†(0.2) *** (****)
Quantitative			13 (0.6) 241 (2.0)	15 (0.8) 234 (5.1)	3 (0.5) 281 (8.3)!	1 (0.5) *** (****)	68 (1.3) 293 (1.9)	0†(0.2) *** (****)
25 to 39 years	10,050	63,278						
Prose			12 (0.3) 251 (2.0)	12 (0.4) 215 (3.5)	2 (0.3) 250 (5.8)!	1 (0.4) 270 (8.7)!	72 (0.8) 303 (0.9)	0†(0.1) *** (****)
Document			12 (0.3) 245 (1.9)	12 (0.4) 216 (3.7)	2 (0.3) 253 (4.8)!	1 (0.4) 268 (8.6)!	72 (0.8) 300 (1.0)	0†(0.1) *** (****)
Quantitative			12 (0.3) 239 (1.9)	12 (0.4) 214 (3.7)	2 (0.3) 263 (5.3)!	1 (0.4) 263 (6.7)!	72 (0.8) 303 (0.9)	0†(0.1) *** (****)
40 to 54 years	6,310	43,794						
Prose			10 (0.3) 235 (2.3)	7 (0.4) 211 (4.5)!	2 (0.2) 248 (7.8)!	1 (0.2) *** (****)	80 (0.5) 300 (1.6)	0†(0.1) *** (****)
Document			10 (0.3) 226 (2.0)	7 (0.4) 208 (4.4)!	2 (0.2) 243 (8.1)!	1 (0.2) *** (****)	80 (0.5) 292 (1.4)	0†(0.1) *** (****)
Quantitative			10 (0.3) 226 (2.6)	7 (0.4) 212 (5.0)!	2 (0.2) 260 (7.4)!	1 (0.2) *** (****)	80 (0.5) 301 (1.4)	0†(0.1) *** (****)
55 to 64 years	2,924	19,503						
Prose			10 (0.5) 212 (4.0)!	8 (0.7) 192 (7.4)!	1 (0.3) *** (****)	1 (0.4) *** (****)	80 (1.1) 273 (2.1)	0†(0.2) *** (****)
Document			10 (0.5) 201 (3.9)!	8 (0.7) 187 (8.2)!	1 (0.3) *** (****)	1 (0.4) *** (****)	80 (1.1) 262 (2.1)	0†(0.2) *** (****)
Quantitative			10 (0.5) 203 (3.9)!	8 (0.7) 195 (8.9)!	1 (0.3) *** (****)	1 (0.4) *** (****)	80 (1.1) 275 (2.3)	0†(0.2) *** (****)
65 years and older	2,214	29,735						
Prose			8 (0.6) 187 (4.5)	5 (0.5) 170 (8.8)!	2 (0.4) *** (****)	1 (0.2) *** (****)	85 (1.0) 240 (2.1)	0†(0.1) *** (****)
Document			8 (0.6) 173 (3.0)	5 (0.5) 151 (6.6)!	2 (0.4) *** (****)	1 (0.2) *** (****)	85 (1.0) 226 (2.1)	0†(0.1) *** (****)
Quantitative			8 (0.6) 163 (5.6)	5 (0.5) 144 (9.6)!	2 (0.4) *** (****)	1 (0.2) *** (****)	85 (1.0) 240 (2.5)	0†(0.1) *** (****)

n = sample size; WGT N = population size estimate / 1,000 (the sample sizes for subpopulations may not add up to the total sample sizes, due to missing data); RPCT = row percentage estimate; PROF = average proficiency estimate; (SE) = standard error of the estimate (the reported sample estimate can be said to be within 2 standard errors of the true population value with 95% confidence).

† Percentages less than 0.5 are rounded to zero.

*** Sample size is insufficient to permit a reliable estimate (fewer than 45 respondents).

! Interpret with caution -- the nature of the sample does not allow accurate determination of the variability of this statistic.

Source: U.S. Department of Education, National Center for Education Statistics, National Adult Literacy Survey, 1992.

TABLE 1.9A

Average Years of Schooling by Age, Race/Ethnicity, and Census Region

DEMOGRAPHIC SUBPOPULATIONS	Average Years of Schooling*	
		(SE)
Age		
16 to 18 years	10.8	(0.1)
19 to 24 years	12.5	(0.0)
25 to 39 years	12.9	(0.0)
40 to 54 years	13.1	(0.1)
55 to 64 years	11.8	(0.1)
65 years and older	10.7	(0.1)
Race/Ethnicity		
Black	11.6	(0.1)
Hispanic	10.2	(0.1)
Asian/Pacific Islander	13.0	(0.3)
American Indian/		
Alaskan Native	11.7	(0.2)
White	12.8	(0.0)
Age by Race/Ethnicity		
16 to 18 years		
White	11.0	(0.2)
Black	10.8	(0.2)
Hispanic	9.9	(0.3)
Asian/Pacific Islander	11.3	(0.9)
19 to 24 years		
White	12.8	(0.0)
Black	12.1	(0.1)
Hispanic	11.4	(0.2)
Asian/Pacific Islander	12.9	(0.3)
25 to 39 years		
White	13.4	(0.0)
Black	12.5	(0.1)
Hispanic	10.5	(0.2)
Asian/Pacific Islander	13.9	(0.3)
40 to 54 years		
White	13.5	(0.1)
Black	11.9	(0.1)
Hispanic	10.3	(0.3)
Asian/Pacific Islander	14.1	(0.5)
55 to 64 years		
White	12.3	(0.1)
Black	10.7	(0.3)
Hispanic	8.8	(0.4)
Asian/Pacific Islander	13.3	(0.9)
65 years and older		
White	11.2	(0.1)
Black	9.0	(0.2)
Hispanic	6.5	(0.4)
Asian/Pacific Islander	8.7	(1.3)

TABLE 1.9A (continued)

Average Years of Schooling by Age, Race/Ethnicity, and Census Region

DEMOGRAPHIC SUBPOPULATIONS	Average Years of Schooling*
	(SE)
Census Region	
Northeast	12.5　(0.1)
Midwest	12.5　(0.1)
South	12.2　(0.1)
West	12.6　(0.1)

*in this country.

n = sample size; WGT N = population size estimate / 1,000 (the sample sizes for subpopulations may not add up to the total sample sizes, due to missing data); (SE) = standard error of the estimate (the reported sample estimate can be said to be within 2 standard errors of the true population value with 95% confidence).

!　Interpret with caution -- the nature of the sample does not allow accurate determination of the variability of this statistic.

Source: U.S. Department of Education, National Center for Education Statistics, National Adult Literacy Survey, 1992.

TABLE 1.9B

Difference in Average Proficiencies and in Average Years of Schooling, by Race/Ethnicity and Age

DEMOGRAPHIC SUBPOPULATIONS	Difference in Average Prose Proficiency	Difference in Average Document Proficiency	Difference in Average Quantitative Proficiency	Difference in Average Years of Schooling
	(SE)	(SE)	(SE)	(SE)
White and Black Adults				
16 to 18 years	36 (4.1)	39 (4.3)	47 (4.5)	.2 (0.3)
19 to 24 years	41 (2.3)	44 (2.4)	52 (2.8)	.7 (0.1)
25 to 39 years	52 (2.2)	55 (2.1)	64 (2.1)	.9 (0.1)
40 to 54 years	65 (2.8)	66 (2.4)	75 (3.0)	1.6 (0.1)
55 to 64 years	61 (4.5)	61 (4.4)	72 (4.5)	1.6 (0.3)
65 years and older	53 (5.0)	53 (3.7)	77 (6.1)	2.2 (0.2)
White and Hispanic Adults				
16 to 18 years	47 (7.0)	50 (6.1)	53 (6.2)	1.1 (0.4)
19 to 24 years	57 (5.1)	57 (5.6)	59 (5.4)	1.4 (0.2)
25 to 39 years	88 (3.6)	84 (3.8)	89 (3.8)	2.9 (0.2)
40 to 54 years	89 (4.8)	84 (4.6)	89 (5.2)	3.2 (0.3)
55 to 64 years	81 (7.7)	75 (8.5)	80 (9.2)	3.5 (0.4)
65 years and older	70 (9.0)	75 (6.9)	96 (9.9)	4.7 (0.4)
White and Asian/				
Pacific Islander Adults				
19 to 24 years	16 (8.7)	17 (8.5)	12 (8.5)	-0.1 (0.3)
25 to 39 years	53 (3.6)	47 (4.9)	40 (5.4)	-0.5 (0.3)
40 to 54 years	52 (8.0)	49 (8.2)	41 (7.5)	-0.6 (0.5)

n = sample size; WGT N = population size estimate / 1,000 (the sample sizes for subpopulations may not add up to the total sample sizes, due to missing data); (SE) = standard error of the estimate (the reported sample estimate can be said to be within 2 standard errors of the true population value with 95% confidence).

!   Interpret with caution -- the nature of the sample does not allow accurate determination of the variability of this statistic.

Source: U.S. Department of Education, National Center for Education Statistics, National Adult Literacy Survey, 1992.

TABLE 1.10

Average Proficiency on Each Literacy Scale
Race/Ethnicity by Country of Birth

RACE/ETHNICITY	COUNTRY OF BIRTH		Born in the USA	Born in Another Country or Territory
	n	WGT N (/1,000)	RPCT (SE) PROF (SE)	RPCT (SE) PROF (SE)
Black	4,963	21,192		
Prose			95 (0.5) 237 (1.4)	6 (0.5) 230 (6.4)
Document			95 (0.5) 230 (1.2)	6 (0.5) 225 (8.7)
Quantitative			95 (0.5) 224 (1.4)	6 (0.5) 227 (7.1)
Hispanic/Mexicano	1,776	10,235		
Prose			54 (2.2) 247 (3.2)	46 (2.2) 158 (3.7)
Document			54 (2.2) 245 (3.0)	46 (2.2) 158 (4.3)
Quantitative			54 (2.2) 244 (3.1)	46 (2.2) 158 (4.5)
Hispanic/Puerto Rican	405	2,190		
Prose			80 (2.9) 226 (6.9)	20 (2.9) 186 (10.3)!
Document			80 (2.9) 225 (6.7)	20 (2.9) 171 (12.4)!
Quantitative			80 (2.9) 223 (6.6)	20 (2.9) 166 (16.0)!
Hispanic/Cuban	147	928		
Prose			11 (2.8) *** (****)	89 (2.8) 202 (10.9)
Document			11 (2.8) *** (****)	89 (2.8) 204 (13.0)
Quantitative			11 (2.8) *** (****)	89 (2.8) 217 (14.6)
Hispanic/Central/South	424	2,608		
Prose			21 (3.1) 281 (6.3)!	79 (3.1) 187 (6.0)
Document			21 (3.1) 277 (5.0)!	79 (3.1) 188 (5.9)
Quantitative			21 (3.1) 275 (5.1)!	79 (3.1) 185 (6.4)
Hispanic/Other	374	2,520		
Prose			68 (5.5) 283 (7.7)	32 (5.5) 210 (10.5)!
Document			68 (5.5) 277 (7.5)	32 (5.5) 204 (11.1)!
Quantitative			68 (5.5) 271 (8.2)	32 (5.5) 191 (13.1)!

n =   sample size; WGT N = population size estimate / 1,000 (the sample sizes for subpopulations may not add up to the total sample sizes, due to missing data); RPCT = row percentage estimate; PROF = average proficiency estimate; (SE) = standard error of the estimate (the reported sample estimate can be said to be within 2 standard errors of the true population value with 95% confidence).

***   Sample size is insufficient to permit a reliable estimate (fewer than 45 respondents).

!   Interpret with caution -- the nature of the sample does not allow accurate determination of the variability of this statistic.

Source: U.S. Department of Education, National Center for Education Statistics, National Adult Literacy Survey, 1992.

TABLE 1.10 (continued)

**Average Proficiency on Each Literacy Scale
Race/Ethnicity by Country of Birth**

RACE/ETHNICITY	COUNTRY OF BIRTH		Born in the USA	Born in Another Country or Territory
	n	WGT N (/1,000)	RPCT (SE) PROF (SE)	RPCT (SE) PROF (SE)
Asian/Pacific Islander	438	4,116		
Prose			22 (2.5) 274 (11.2)!	78 (2.5) 233 (7.2)
Document			22 (2.5) 266 (12.4)!	78 (2.5) 240 (5.4)
Quantitative			22 (2.5) 279 (10.0)!	78 (2.5) 249 (7.9)
American Indian/Alaskan Native	189	1,803		
Prose			100 (0.4) 254 (4.1)!	0†(0.4) *** (****)
Document			100 (0.4) 254 (5.0)!	0†(0.4) *** (****)
Quantitative			100 (0.4) 250 (5.1)!	0†(0.4) *** (****)
White	17,292	144,968		
Prose			96 (0.2) 287 (0.8)	4 (0.2) 258 (4.3)
Document			96 (0.2) 281 (0.9)	4 (0.2) 255 (3.3)
Quantitative			96 (0.2) 288 (0.8)	4 (0.2) 260 (4.2)
Other	83	729		
Prose			24 (7.8) *** (****)	76 (7.8) 197 (16.3)
Document			24 (7.8) *** (****)	76 (7.8) 203 (15.5)
Quantitative			24 (7.8) *** (****)	76 (7.8) 202 (12.3)

n = sample size; WGT N = population size estimate / 1,000 (the sample sizes for subpopulations may not add up to the total sample sizes, due to missing data); RPCT = row percentage estimate; PROF = average proficiency estimate; (SE) = standard error of the estimate (the reported sample estimate can be said to be within 2 standard errors of the true population value with 95% confidence).

† Percentages less than 0.5 are rounded to zero.
*** Sample size is insufficient to permit a reliable estimate (fewer than 45 respondents).
! Interpret with caution -- the nature of the sample does not allow accurate determination of the variability of this statistic.

Source: U.S. Department of Education, National Center for Education Statistics, National Adult Literacy Survey, 1992.

TABLE 1.11

Average Proficiency on Each Literacy Scale
Census Region by Country of Birth

CENSUS REGION	COUNTRY OF BIRTH		Born in the USA	Born in Another Country or Territory
		n	WGT N (/1,000)	RPCT (SE) / PROF (SE)	RPCT (SE) / PROF (SE)

CENSUS REGION	COUNTRY OF BIRTH	n	WGT N (/1,000)	Born in the USA RPCT (SE) PROF (SE)	Born in Another Country or Territory RPCT (SE) PROF (SE)
Northeast		5,425	39,834		
	Prose			86 (0.7) / 279 (1.3)	14 (0.7) / 213 (3.3)
	Document			86 (0.7) / 272 (1.4)	14 (0.7) / 210 (3.4)
	Quantitative			86 (0.7) / 276 (1.3)	14 (0.7) / 211 (4.5)
Midwest		7,494	45,318		
	Prose			97 (0.3) / 281 (1.1)	3 (0.3) / 223 (7.9)
	Document			97 (0.3) / 275 (1.3)	3 (0.3) / 227 (8.5)
	Quantitative			97 (0.3) / 281 (1.7)	3 (0.3) / 229 (9.3)
South		7,886	65,854		
	Prose			93 (0.5) / 271 (2.1)	7 (0.5) / 219 (4.2)
	Document			93 (0.5) / 265 (2.1)	7 (0.5) / 219 (4.5)
	Quantitative			93 (0.5) / 269 (2.2)	7 (0.5) / 224 (4.5)
West		5,286	40,282		
	Prose			82 (0.9) / 292 (1.9)	18 (0.9) / 204 (5.0)
	Document			82 (0.9) / 285 (1.7)	18 (0.9) / 204 (4.9)
	Quantitative			82 (0.9) / 290 (1.9)	18 (0.9) / 208 (5.9)

n = sample size; WGT N = population size estimate / 1,000 (the sample sizes for subpopulations may not add up to the total sample sizes, due to missing data); RPCT = row percentage estimate; PROF = average proficiency estimate; (SE) = standard error of the estimate (the reported sample estimate can be said to be within 2 standard errors of the true population value with 95% confidence).

Source: U.S. Department of Education, National Center for Education Statistics, National Adult Literacy Survey, 1992.

TABLE 1.12A

Average Prose Proficiency and Literacy Levels
by Type of Physical, Mental, or Health Condition

DISABILITIES	PROSE SCALE		Level 1 225 or lower	Level 2 226 to 275	Level 3 276 to 325	Level 4 326 to 375	Level 5 376 or higher	Overall Proficiency
	n	WGT N (/1,000)	RPCT (SE)	RPCT (SE)	RPCT (SE)	RPCT (SE)	RPCT (SE)	PROF (SE)
Physical, Mental, Health Condition Yes	2,806	22,205	46 (1.1)	30 (1.6)	18 (1.5)	5 (0.9)	1 (0.2)	227 (1.6)
Visual Difficulty Yes	1,801	14,296	54 (1.6)	26 (1.4)	15 (1.6)	5 (1.3)	0†(0.2)	217 (2.4)
Hearing Difficulty Yes	1,611	14,202	36 (1.9)	30 (2.0)	24 (1.9)	9 (1.4)	1 (0.4)	243 (2.6)
Learning Disability Yes	875	5,820	58 (2.4)	22 (2.4)	14 (1.6)	4 (1.1)	1 (0.6)	207 (3.7)
Mental or Emotional Condition Yes	597	3,631	48 (3.2)	24 (2.7)	18 (2.3)	8 (1.8)	2 (0.9)	225 (4.8)
Mental Retardation Yes	63	370	87 (6.0)	3 (4.4)	5 (4.1)	3 (3.2)	1 (1.7)	143 (13.6)
Speech Disability Yes	383	2,767	53 (4.0)	26 (3.8)	13 (2.7)	7 (2.4)	0†(0.4)	216 (6.6)
Physical Disability Yes	2,129	17,144	44 (1.3)	30 (1.5)	19 (1.6)	6 (1.0)	1 (0.2)	231 (1.8)
Long-term Illness 6 months or more Yes	1,880	14,627	41 (1.5)	29 (1.3)	21 (1.4)	7 (1.1)	1 (0.4)	236 (2.4)
Any Other Health Impairment Yes	1,509	12,058	39 (2.1)	30 (2.7)	23 (2.2)	7 (1.2)	1 (0.3)	237 (2.6)

n = sample size; WGT N = population size estimate / 1,000 (the sample sizes for subpopulations may not add up to the total sample sizes, due to missing data); RPCT = row percentage estimate; PROF = average proficiency estimate; (SE) = standard error of the estimate (the reported sample estimate can be said to be within 2 standard errors of the true population value with 95% confidence).

† Percentages less than 0.5 are rounded to zero.

Source: U.S. Department of Education, National Center for Education Statistics, National Adult Literacy Survey, 1992.

TABLE 1.12B

Average Document Proficiency and Literacy Levels by Type of Physical, Mental, or Health Condition

DISABILITIES	DOCUMENT SCALE		Level 1 225 or lower	Level 2 226 to 275	Level 3 276 to 325	Level 4 326 to 375	Level 5 376 or higher	Overall Proficiency
	n	WGT N (/1,000)	RPCT (SE)	RPCT (SE)	RPCT (SE)	RPCT (SE)	RPCT (SE)	PROF (SE)
Physical, Mental, Health Condition Yes	2,532	19,859	49 (1.4)	30 (1.3)	16 (1.1)	5 (0.6)	1 (0.3)	222 (2.0)
Visual Difficulty Yes	1,613	12,628	55 (1.7)	26 (2.3)	14 (2.1)	5 (0.9)	1 (0.3)	215 (2.7)
Hearing Difficulty Yes	1,483	12,876	37 (2.3)	31 (2.1)	23 (1.7)	8 (1.1)	1 (0.4)	239 (3.1)
Learning Disability Yes	812	5,421	60 (2.7)	22 (3.1)	13 (1.5)	4 (1.1)	1 (1.0)	203 (4.3)
Mental or Emotional Condition Yes	527	3,171	45 (3.4)	28 (3.0)	17 (2.5)	8 (2.1)	2 (0.8)	224 (5.2)
Mental Retardation Yes	54	346	86 (6.8)	5 (5.3)	6 (3.3)	3 (2.8)	0[†](0.7)	147 (14.0)
Speech Disability Yes	342	2,402	55 (4.3)	27 (4.4)	13 (2.5)	5 (1.8)	1 (0.5)	213 (5.6)
Physical Disability Yes	1,892	15,164	47 (1.4)	29 (1.5)	18 (1.6)	6 (0.7)	0[†](0.1)	226 (2.1)
Long-term Illness 6 months or more Yes	1,652	12,687	44 (1.9)	31 (2.5)	19 (1.8)	6 (0.9)	1 (0.4)	230 (2.6)
Any Other Health Impairment Yes	1,332	10,572	43 (2.4)	31 (2.6)	20 (2.0)	6 (1.2)	1 (0.3)	231 (2.5)

n = sample size; WGT N = population size estimate / 1,000 (the sample sizes for subpopulations may not add up to the total sample sizes, due to missing data); RPCT = row percentage estimate; PROF = average proficiency estimate; (SE) = standard error of the estimate (the reported sample estimate can be said to be within 2 standard errors of the true population value with 95% confidence).

† Percentages less than 0.5 are rounded to zero.

Source: U.S. Department of Education, National Center for Education Statistics, National Adult Literacy Survey, 1992.

TABLE 1.12C

Average Quantitative Proficiency and Literacy Levels by Type of Physical, Mental, or Health Condition

DISABILITIES	QUANTITATIVE SCALE		Level 1 225 or lower	Level 2 226 to 275	Level 3 276 to 325	Level 4 326 to 375	Level 5 376 or higher	Overall Proficiency
	n	WGT N (/1,000)	RPCT (SE)	RPCT (SE)	RPCT (SE)	RPCT (SE)	RPCT (SE)	PROF (SE)
Physical, Mental, Health Condition Yes	2,532	19,859	47 (1.3)	26 (1.3)	20 (1.4)	6 (0.7)	1 (0.4)	224 (2.5)
Visual Difficulty Yes	1,613	12,628	53 (1.8)	24 (1.8)	16 (1.6)	5 (1.2)	1 (0.5)	214 (2.6)
Hearing Difficulty Yes	1,483	12,876	34 (2.5)	25 (1.9)	27 (1.9)	11 (1.7)	2 (0.7)	247 (3.9)
Learning Disability Yes	812	5,421	60 (3.2)	21 (2.5)	14 (1.6)	4 (1.3)	1 (0.6)	200 (4.4)
Mental or Emotional Condition Yes	527	3,171	51 (3.7)	23 (2.9)	17 (2.6)	8 (2.0)	2 (1.3)	215 (6.7)
Mental Retardation Yes	54	346	89 (4.6)	4 (4.0)	6 (5.2)	1 (1.0)	0†(1.7)	117 (15.2)
Speech Disability Yes	342	2,402	54 (3.7)	22 (3.6)	17 (3.0)	6 (2.6)	1 (1.0)	212 (7.7)
Physical Disability Yes	1,892	15,164	45 (1.8)	26 (1.7)	21 (1.3)	7 (0.9)	1 (0.3)	228 (2.4)
Long-term Illness 6 months or more Yes	1,652	12,687	41 (1.6)	25 (1.6)	24 (2.1)	8 (1.0)	2 (0.4)	233 (2.9)
Any Other Health Impairment Yes	1,332	10,572	38 (2.1)	26 (2.0)	24 (2.0)	9 (1.4)	2 (0.7)	239 (3.3)

n = sample size; WGT N = population size estimate / 1,000 (the sample sizes for subpopulations may not add up to the total sample sizes, due to missing data); RPCT = row percentage estimate; PROF = average proficiency estimate; (SE) = standard error of the estimate (the reported sample estimate can be said to be within 2 standard errors of the true population value with 95% confidence).

† Percentages less than 0.5 are rounded to zero.

Source: U.S. Department of Education, National Center for Education Statistics, National Adult Literacy Survey, 1992.

TABLE 2.1A

Newspaper Reading Practices, Help from Others, and English Literacy by Prose Literacy Levels

NEWSPAPER READING PRACTICES, HELP FROM OTHERS, ENGLISH LITERACY	PROSE SCALE		Level 1 225 or lower	Level 2 226 to 275	Level 3 276 to 325	Level 4 326 to 375	Level 5 376 or higher	Overall Proficiency
	n	WGT N (/1,000)	CPCT (SE)	CPCT (SE)	CPCT (SE)	CPCT (SE)	CPCT (SE)	PROF (SE)
Newspaper Reading								
Every day	12,157	93,536	35 (0.5)	49 (0.9)	52 (0.7)	57 (1.2)	61 (3.1)	285 (0.7)
A few times a week	6,482	45,127	19 (0.8)	24 (1.1)	25 (1.0)	25 (1.2)	25 (3.1)	280 (1.2)
Once a week	3,675	27,075	16 (0.9)	15 (1.0)	14 (1.2)	12 (1.0)	8 (1.3)	267 (1.4)
Less than once a week	2,076	13,923	9 (1.5)	8 (1.4)	6 (1.6)	5 (1.1)	5 (1.0)	259 (2.3)
Never	1,686	11,511	21 (1.5)	3 (1.2)	2 (0.9)	1 (0.6)	1 (0.2)	174 (2.8)
Read News, Editorials								
No	870	6,574	8 (2.4)	5 (2.6)	3 (1.9)	1 (1.1)	0[†](0.3)	248 (2.7)
Yes	21,444	159,164	92 (0.5)	95 (0.6)	97 (0.5)	99 (0.4)	100 (0.3)	282 (0.6)
Read Sports								
No	11,641	85,383	52 (0.7)	53 (1.2)	52 (1.2)	50 (1.1)	47 (2.4)	280 (0.8)
Yes	10,673	80,355	48 (0.7)	47 (1.3)	48 (1.2)	50 (1.1)	53 (2.4)	282 (0.8)
Read Home, Fashion								
No	3,788	30,892	26 (1.0)	20 (1.3)	17 (1.3)	14 (0.9)	14 (0.7)	267 (1.6)
Yes	18,526	134,846	74 (0.7)	80 (0.7)	83 (0.6)	86 (0.7)	86 (0.7)	284 (0.5)
Read Ads, Listings								
No	2,918	23,564	16 (1.1)	12 (1.3)	13 (1.2)	17 (1.1)	24 (1.9)	282 (1.7)
Yes	19,396	142,174	84 (0.7)	88 (0.6)	87 (0.8)	83 (0.6)	76 (1.8)	280 (0.6)
Read Comics, Advice								
No	6,300	48,452	34 (1.1)	28 (1.0)	28 (1.1)	29 (0.7)	31 (1.7)	277 (1.3)
Yes	16,014	117,286	66 (1.0)	72 (0.8)	72 (0.8)	71 (0.5)	69 (1.7)	282 (0.6)
English Reading Ability								
Very well/well	24,135	177,713	71 (0.4)	97 (0.6)	99 (0.5)	100 (0.4)	100 (0.2)	282 (0.5)
Not well/not at all	1,906	13,214	29 (1.5)	3 (1.2)	1 (0.7)	0[†](0.2)	0[†](0.0)	150 (2.6)
English Writing Ability								
Very well/well	23,455	172,519	66 (0.4)	94 (0.6)	98 (0.5)	99 (0.4)	100 (0.2)	283 (0.6)
Not well/not at all	2,544	18,129	34 (1.4)	6 (1.1)	2 (0.8)	1 (0.2)	0[†](0.1)	174 (2.4)
Help With Forms								
A lot	2,763	23,034	27 (1.4)	12 (1.2)	8 (1.2)	4 (0.6)	2 (0.5)	221 (2.2)
Some/None	23,294	168,062	73 (0.4)	88 (0.6)	92 (0.5)	96 (0.4)	98 (0.5)	280 (0.6)
Help With Information								
A lot	2,230	17,123	23 (1.4)	8 (1.2)	5 (1.3)	2 (0.6)	1 (0.4)	210 (2.5)
Some/None	23,790	173,731	77 (0.4)	92 (0.6)	95 (0.5)	98 (0.4)	99 (0.4)	279 (0.6)
Help With Basic Math								
A lot	1,219	9,293	15 (1.8)	4 (1.8)	2 (1.1)	1 (0.7)	0[†](0.2)	192 (3.2)
Some/None	24,835	181,761	85 (0.4)	96 (0.7)	98 (0.5)	99 (0.4)	100 (0.2)	277 (0.5)

n = sample size; WGT N = population size estimate / 1,000 (the sample sizes for subpopulations may not add up to the total sample sizes, due to missing data); CPCT = column percentage estimate; PROF = average proficiency estimate; (SE) = standard error of the estimate (the reported sample estimate can be said to be within 2 standard errors of the true population value with 95% confidence).

[†] Percentages less than 0.5 are rounded to zero.

Source: U.S. Department of Education, National Center for Education Statistics, National Adult Literacy Survey, 1992.

TABLE 2.1B

Newspaper Reading Practices, Help from Others, and English Literacy by Document Literacy Levels

NEWSPAPER READING PRACTICES, HELP FROM OTHERS, ENGLISH LITERACY	DOCUMENT SCALE		Level 1 225 or lower	Level 2 226 to 275	Level 3 276 to 325	Level 4 326 to 375	Level 5 376 or higher	Overall Proficiency
	n	WGT N (/1,000)	CPCT (SE)	CPCT (SE)	CPCT (SE)	CPCT (SE)	CPCT (SE)	PROF (SE)
Newspaper Reading								
Every day	12,157	93,536	39 (0.6)	51 (0.8)	51 (0.9)	55 (1.4)	55 (1.8)	276 (0.8)
A few times a week	6,482	45,127	18 (0.6)	24 (0.8)	26 (0.9)	26 (1.2)	28 (2.3)	277 (1.2)
Once a week	3,675	27,075	15 (1.1)	15 (0.9)	14 (1.2)	12 (0.9)	11 (1.4)	265 (1.4)
Less than once a week	2,076	13,923	9 (1.5)	8 (1.2)	7 (1.6)	6 (1.4)	6 (1.2)	257 (2.2)
Never	1,686	11,511	19 (1.5)	3 (1.2)	2 (1.0)	1 (0.4)	1 (0.4)	170 (2.9)
Read News, Editorials								
No	870	6,574	7 (1.9)	4 (2.4)	3 (2.2)	2 (0.9)	1 (0.5)	248 (3.1)
Yes	21,444	159,164	93 (0.5)	96 (0.5)	97 (0.5)	98 (0.6)	99 (0.4)	276 (0.6)
Read Sports								
No	11,641	85,383	53 (0.9)	53 (0.7)	51 (0.8)	49 (1.4)	47 (0.9)	273 (0.9)
Yes	10,673	80,355	47 (1.0)	47 (0.8)	49 (0.9)	51 (1.4)	53 (0.9)	276 (1.0)
Read Home, Fashion								
No	3,788	30,892	24 (1.1)	19 (1.1)	17 (1.3)	15 (1.1)	15 (1.1)	264 (1.6)
Yes	18,526	134,846	76 (0.6)	81 (0.8)	83 (0.6)	85 (1.0)	85 (1.0)	277 (0.6)
Read Ads, Listings								
No	2,918	23,564	16 (1.1)	12 (1.1)	13 (1.2)	17 (1.1)	22 (1.8)	274 (1.7)
Yes	19,396	142,174	84 (0.5)	88 (0.6)	87 (0.7)	83 (0.7)	78 (1.7)	274 (0.6)
Read Comics, Advice								
No	6,300	48,452	33 (0.9)	27 (0.7)	29 (1.1)	28 (1.1)	30 (2.2)	271 (1.2)
Yes	16,014	117,286	67 (0.7)	73 (0.6)	71 (0.8)	72 (0.9)	70 (2.2)	276 (0.7)
English Reading Ability								
Very well/well	24,135	177,713	75 (0.4)	97 (0.5)	99 (0.5)	100 (0.4)	100 (0.1)	276 (0.6)
Not well/not at all	1,906	13,214	25 (1.3)	3 (1.0)	1 (0.6)	0†(0.4)	0†(0.0)	151 (2.6)
English Writing Ability								
Very well/well	23,455	172,519	70 (0.4)	94 (0.4)	97 (0.5)	99 (0.4)	100 (0.3)	277 (0.6)
Not well/not at all	2,544	18,129	30 (1.6)	6 (1.3)	3 (0.7)	1 (0.2)	0†(0.3)	175 (2.4)
Help With Forms								
A lot	2,763	23,034	25 (1.3)	12 (1.4)	7 (0.8)	4 (0.7)	2 (0.4)	217 (2.0)
Some/None	23,294	168,062	75 (0.5)	88 (0.6)	93 (0.5)	96 (0.5)	98 (0.4)	274 (0.6)
Help With Information								
A lot	2,230	17,123	21 (1.3)	8 (1.2)	5 (0.9)	2 (0.6)	1 (0.4)	206 (2.3)
Some/None	23,790	173,731	79 (0.5)	92 (0.4)	95 (0.4)	98 (0.5)	99 (0.4)	273 (0.6)
Help With Basic Math								
A lot	1,219	9,293	14 (1.4)	4 (1.2)	2 (1.1)	1 (0.5)	0†(0.2)	187 (2.9)
Some/None	24,835	181,761	86 (0.5)	96 (0.4)	98 (0.4)	99 (0.4)	100 (0.2)	271 (0.6)

n = sample size; WGT N = population size estimate / 1,000 (the sample sizes for subpopulations may not add up to the total sample sizes, due to missing data); CPCT = column percentage estimate; PROF = average proficiency estimate; (SE) = standard error of the estimate (the reported sample estimate can be said to be within 2 standard errors of the true population value with 95% confidence).

† Percentages less than 0.5 are rounded to zero.

Source: U.S. Department of Education, National Center for Education Statistics, National Adult Literacy Survey, 1992.

TABLE 2.1C

Newspaper Reading Practices, Help from Others, and English Literacy by Quantitative Literacy Levels

NEWSPAPER READING PRACTICES, HELP FROM OTHERS, ENGLISH LITERACY	QUANTITATIVE SCALE		Level 1 225 or lower	Level 2 226 to 275	Level 3 276 to 325	Level 4 326 to 375	Level 5 376 or higher	Overall Proficiency
	n	WGT N (/1,000)	CPCT (SE)	CPCT (SE)	CPCT (SE)	CPCT (SE)	CPCT (SE)	PROF (SE)
Newspaper Reading								
Every day	12,157	93,536	35 (0.6)	48 (0.8)	52 (0.8)	58 (0.8)	62 (2.0)	285 (0.9)
A few times a week	6,482	45,127	20 (0.6)	25 (1.0)	25 (0.8)	24 (0.8)	23 (1.7)	278 (1.2)
Once a week	3,675	27,075	16 (1.1)	15 (0.9)	14 (0.9)	11 (0.8)	9 (0.9)	266 (1.5)
Less than once a week	2,076	13,923	9 (1.4)	8 (1.5)	7 (1.2)	5 (1.0)	5 (1.0)	258 (2.4)
Never	1,686	11,511	20 (1.5)	4 (1.3)	2 (0.9)	1 (0.7)	1 (0.3)	163 (2.9)
Read News, Editorials								
No	870	6,574	7 (1.8)	5 (1.7)	3 (1.8)	2 (1.1)	1 (0.6)	250 (2.8)
Yes	21,444	159,164	93 (0.4)	95 (0.4)	97 (0.5)	98 (0.4)	99 (0.5)	281 (0.7)
Read Sports								
No	11,641	85,383	55 (0.7)	54 (0.9)	51 (0.7)	47 (1.0)	42 (2.2)	276 (1.0)
Yes	10,673	80,355	45 (0.7)	46 (0.8)	49 (0.8)	53 (1.0)	58 (2.2)	284 (0.9)
Read Home, Fashion								
No	3,788	30,892	23 (1.2)	18 (0.9)	18 (1.3)	17 (1.1)	17 (1.3)	271 (1.7)
Yes	18,526	134,846	77 (0.6)	82 (0.7)	82 (0.5)	83 (0.8)	83 (1.3)	282 (0.7)
Read Ads, Listings								
No	2,918	23,564	16 (1.0)	12 (1.2)	12 (0.9)	17 (1.0)	23 (1.6)	282 (1.9)
Yes	19,396	142,174	84 (0.6)	88 (0.7)	88 (0.5)	83 (0.5)	77 (1.5)	280 (0.7)
Read Comics, Advice								
No	6,300	48,452	32 (0.7)	27 (0.8)	28 (0.9)	30 (0.9)	33 (1.6)	279 (1.1)
Yes	16,014	117,286	68 (0.5)	73 (0.6)	72 (0.5)	70 (0.9)	67 (1.5)	280 (0.7)
English Reading Ability								
Very well/well	24,135	177,713	74 (0.4)	97 (0.5)	99 (0.5)	100 (0.3)	100 (0.2)	281 (0.6)
Not well/not at all	1,906	13,214	26 (1.5)	3 (0.9)	1 (0.9)	0† (0.3)	0† (0.1)	148 (2.6)
English Writing Ability								
Very well/well	23,455	172,519	70 (0.4)	93 (0.5)	97 (0.5)	99 (0.3)	100 (0.2)	282 (0.7)
Not well/not at all	2,544	18,129	30 (1.4)	7 (1.1)	3 (0.9)	1 (0.4)	0† (0.2)	173 (2.7)
Help With Forms								
A lot	2,763	23,034	26 (1.6)	12 (1.6)	7 (0.9)	4 (0.7)	2 (0.2)	216 (2.3)
Some/None	23,294	168,062	74 (0.5)	88 (0.9)	93 (0.6)	96 (0.5)	98 (0.2)	279 (0.7)
Help With Information								
A lot	2,230	17,123	22 (1.5)	8 (1.3)	5 (0.9)	3 (0.8)	1 (0.5)	201 (2.8)
Some/None	23,790	173,731	78 (0.4)	92 (0.6)	95 (0.5)	97 (0.5)	99 (0.5)	278 (0.6)
Help With Basic Math								
A lot	1,219	9,293	14 (1.7)	4 (1.4)	2 (1.3)	1 (0.6)	0† (0.2)	181 (3.2)
Some/None	24,835	181,761	86 (0.4)	96 (0.4)	98 (0.4)	99 (0.3)	100 (0.3)	276 (0.7)

n = sample size; WGT N = population size estimate / 1,000 (the sample sizes for subpopulations may not add up to the total sample sizes, due to missing data); CPCT = column percentage estimate; PROF = average proficiency estimate; (SE) = standard error of the estimate (the reported sample estimate can be said to be within 2 standard errors of the true population value with 95% confidence).

† Percentages less than 0.5 are rounded to zero.

Source: U.S. Department of Education, National Center for Education Statistics, National Adult Literacy Survey, 1992.

TABLE 2.2A

Labor Status, Sources of Information, Voting, and Occupation by Prose Literacy Levels

LABOR STATUS, INFORMATION, VOTING AND OCCUPATION	PROSE SCALE		Level 1 225 or lower	Level 2 226 to 275	Level 3 276 to 325	Level 4 326 to 375	Level 5 376 or higher	Overall Proficiency
	n	WGT N (/1,000)	CPCT (SE)	CPCT (SE)	CPCT (SE)	CPCT (SE)	CPCT (SE)	PROF (SE)
Labor Force Status								
Full-time employed	12,466	89,723	30 (0.9)	43 (0.9)	54 (0.9)	64 (1.2)	72 (1.9)	288 (0.9)
Part-time employed	3,051	23,600	9 (0.7)	12 (1.4)	15 (1.4)	15 (1.1)	14 (0.9)	284 (1.4)
Unemployed	1,942	13,557	8 (1.1)	10 (1.4)	7 (1.7)	4 (1.2)	3 (0.7)	260 (2.1)
Out of labor force	6,721	58,202	52 (0.9)	35 (1.0)	25 (1.0)	17 (1.1)	11 (1.7)	246 (1.1)
Info. from Newspapers or Magazines								
A lot or some	20,842	159,870	68 (0.4)	85 (0.8)	89 (0.7)	91 (0.5)	92 (1.3)	280 (0.5)
A little or none	4,086	30,549	32 (1.2)	15 (1.1)	11 (1.1)	9 (0.8)	8 (1.3)	234 (1.7)
Info. from Radio or Television								
A lot or some	23,955	182,599	94 (0.4)	97 (0.6)	97 (0.5)	96 (0.5)	93 (1.7)	273 (0.6)
A little or none	973	7,822	6 (2.1)	3 (1.7)	3 (1.8)	4 (1.9)	7 (2.0)	257 (4.0)
Info. from Family								
A lot or some	16,710	126,593	62 (0.7)	66 (0.7)	69 (0.7)	69 (0.6)	67 (1.8)	275 (0.8)
A little or none	8,191	63,633	38 (0.8)	34 (0.8)	31 (0.7)	31 (0.7)	33 (1.9)	268 (1.2)
Voted in the Past Five Years								
Yes	15,484	117,379	55 (0.6)	61 (0.9)	69 (0.6)	81 (0.8)	89 (1.2)	285 (0.7)
No	7,616	58,510	45 (0.8)	39 (1.1)	31 (0.7)	19 (0.8)	11 (1.2)	257 (1.0)
Most Recent Occupation								
Prof/Managers	5,461	35,599	5 (0.5)	12 (0.9)	23 (0.8)	40 (1.1)	70 (2.6)	322 (1.0)
Saloo	6,544	41,713	15 (0.6)	28 (0.9)	34 (0.9)	30 (1.0)	20 (2.1)	293 (1.1)
Craft	5,614	42,187	43 (1.0)	36 (1.1)	27 (1.0)	17 (0.8)	8 (1.4)	264 (1.1)
Laborer	3,479	27,671	37 (1.3)	24 (1.3)	16 (1.1)	7 (0.7)	2 (0.5)	249 (1.8)

n = sample size; WGT N = population size estimate / 1,000 (the sample sizes for subpopulations may not add up to the total sample sizes, due to missing data); CPCT = column percentage estimate; PROF = average proficiency estimate; (SE) = standard error of the estimate (the reported sample estimate can be said to be within 2 standard errors of the true population value with 95% confidence).

Source: U.S. Department of Education, National Center for Education Statistics, National Adult Literacy Survey, 1992.

TABLE 2.2B

Labor Status, Sources of Information, Voting, and Occupation by Document Literacy Levels

LABOR STATUS, INFORMATION, VOTING AND OCCUPATION	DOCUMENT SCALE		Level 1 225 or lower	Level 2 226 to 275	Level 3 276 to 325	Level 4 326 to 375	Level 5 376 or higher	Overall Proficiency
	n	WGT N (/1,000)	CPCT (SE)	CPCT (SE)	CPCT (SE)	CPCT (SE)	CPCT (SE)	PROF (SE)
Labor Force Status								
Full-time employed	12,466	89,723	29 (0.8)	44 (0.6)	56 (0.7)	66 (1.0)	74 (1.0)	284 (0.9)
Part-time employed	3,051	23,600	9 (0.8)	13 (1.1)	14 (1.3)	14 (1.0)	13 (0.7)	277 (1.3)
Unemployed	1,942	13,557	8 (1.1)	9 (1.3)	7 (1.3)	5 (0.9)	4 (0.9)	257 (1.8)
Out of labor force	6,721	58,202	53 (1.1)	34 (0.8)	23 (0.8)	15 (0.8)	10 (0.5)	237 (1.3)
Info. from Newspapers or Magazines								
A lot or some	20,842	159,870	71 (0.5)	86 (0.5)	89 (0.5)	90 (0.5)	89 (0.9)	274 (0.6)
A little or none	4,086	30,549	29 (1.2)	14 (0.8)	11 (0.9)	10 (0.7)	11 (0.9)	232 (1.8)
Info. from Radio or Television								
A lot or some	23,955	182,599	94 (0.4)	97 (0.4)	96 (0.5)	96 (0.4)	94 (1.2)	268 (0.7)
A little or none	973	7,822	6 (2.2)	3 (2.0)	4 (1.8)	4 (1.2)	6 (1.3)	252 (3.4)
Info. from Family								
A lot or some	16,710	126,593	62 (0.6)	67 (0.8)	69 (0.9)	69 (0.5)	65 (2.2)	269 (0.9)
A little or none	8,191	63,633	38 (0.7)	33 (0.9)	31 (0.9)	31 (0.5)	35 (2.2)	263 (1.1)
Voted in the Past Five Years								
Yes	15,484	117,379	58 (0.6)	63 (0.6)	68 (0.6)	78 (0.7)	86 (1.8)	277 (0.8)
No	7,616	58,510	42 (0.6)	37 (0.8)	32 (0.7)	22 (0.7)	14 (1.8)	255 (1.0)
Most Recent Occupation								
Prof/Managers	5,461	35,599	6 (0.8)	13 (0.8)	26 (1.1)	46 (1.3)	66 (2.1)	315 (1.0)
Sales	6,544	41,713	16 (0.7)	30 (0.8)	33 (1.2)	29 (1.4)	19 (1.2)	287 (1.0)
Craft	5,614	42,187	41 (0.7)	34 (1.0)	26 (1.1)	18 (1.0)	10 (1.2)	262 (1.2)
Laborer	3,479	27,671	36 (1.5)	23 (1.3)	15 (1.2)	8 (0.6)	4 (0.9)	247 (1.7)

n = sample size; WGT N = population size estimate / 1,000 (the sample sizes for subpopulations may not add up to the total sample sizes, due to missing data); CPCT = column percentage estimate; PROF = average proficiency estimate; (SE) = standard error of the estimate (the reported sample estimate can be said to be within 2 standard errors of the true population value with 95% confidence).

Source: U.S. Department of Education, National Center for Education Statistics, National Adult Literacy Survey, 1992.

TABLE 2.2C

Labor Status, Sources of Information, Voting, and Occupation by Quantitative Literacy Levels

NEWSPAPER READING, INFORMATION, VOTING AND OCCUPATION	QUANTITATIVE SCALE		Level 1 225 or lower	Level 2 226 to 275	Level 3 276 to 325	Level 4 326 to 375	Level 5 376 or higher	Overall Proficiency
	n	WGT N (/1,000)	CPCT (SE)	CPCT (SE)	CPCT (SE)	CPCT (SE)	CPCT (SE)	PROF (SE)
Labor Force Status								
Full-time employed	12,466	89,723	29 (0.7)	43 (0.9)	55 (1.0)	64 (1.1)	73 (1.0)	290 (0.9)
Part-time employed	3,051	23,600	9 (0.9)	14 (1.2)	15 (1.4)	13 (1.1)	11 (0.8)	280 (1.5)
Unemployed	1,942	13,557	9 (1.2)	9 (1.4)	6 (1.5)	4 (1.0)	3 (0.5)	256 (1.9)
Out of labor force	6,721	58,202	53 (1.0)	34 (0.8)	24 (0.8)	18 (1.1)	13 (1.4)	241 (1.6)
Info. from Newspapers or Magazines								
A lot or some	20,842	159,870	70 (0.5)	85 (0.5)	88 (0.5)	90 (0.5)	90 (1.3)	279 (0.6)
A little or none	4,086	30,549	30 (1.1)	15 (1.0)	12 (1.3)	10 (0.8)	10 (1.3)	231 (2.1)
Info. from Radio or Television								
A lot or some	23,955	182,599	94 (0.5)	97 (0.5)	97 (0.4)	96 (0.3)	94 (0.9)	272 (0.7)
A little or none	973	7,822	6 (1.9)	3 (1.7)	3 (1.9)	4 (1.7)	6 (1.2)	257 (4.2)
Info. from Family								
A lot or some	16,710	126,593	63 (0.7)	67 (0.8)	68 (0.8)	67 (0.9)	62 (1.2)	273 (1.0)
A little or none	8,191	63,633	37 (0.9)	33 (0.8)	32 (0.8)	33 (1.0)	38 (1.2)	269 (1.3)
Voted in the Past Five Years								
Yes	15,484	117,379	55 (0.5)	61 (0.6)	69 (0.6)	79 (0.6)	88 (1.6)	284 (1.0)
No	7,616	58,510	45 (0.7)	39 (0.8)	31 (0.8)	21 (0.5)	12 (1.6)	255 (1.1)
Most Recent Occupation								
Prof/Managers	5,461	35,600	0 (0.6)	13 (0.9)	24 (1.0)	43 (0.8)	65 (1.5)	322 (1.0)
Sales	6,544	41,713	16 (0.6)	29 (0.8)	34 (1.2)	29 (1.3)	20 (0.8)	292 (1.1)
Craft	5,614	42,187	43 (1.1)	35 (1.0)	27 (1.1)	18 (0.8)	10 (1.7)	264 (1.3)
Laborer	3,479	27,671	34 (1.4)	23 (1.4)	16 (1.3)	10 (1.3)	5 (0.7)	253 (2.0)

n = sample size; WGT N = population size estimate / 1,000 (the sample sizes for subpopulations may not add up to the total sample sizes, due to missing data); CPCT = column percentage estimate; PROF = average proficiency estimate; (SE) = standard error of the estimate (the reported sample estimate can be said to be within 2 standard errors of the true population value with 95% confidence).

Source: U.S. Department of Education, National Center for Education Statistics, National Adult Literacy Survey, 1992.

TABLE 2.3

Average Proficiency on Each Literacy Scale and Literacy Levels by Poverty Level and Sources of Nonwage Income

SUBPOPULATIONS BASED ON POVERTY LEVEL AND NONWAGE INCOME SOURCES	LITERACY LEVELS		Level 1 225 or lower	Level 2 226 to 275	Level 3 276 to 325	Level 4 326 to 375	Level 5 376 or higher	Overall Proficiency
	n	WGT N (/1,000)	CPCT (SE)	CPCT (SE)	CPCT (SE)	CPCT (SE)	CPCT (SE)	PROF (SE)
Prose								
Poverty Level								
Not poor	14,868	113,929	57 (0.4)	77 (0.8)	88 (0.6)	92 (0.5)	96 (0.8)	290 (0.7)
Poor/near poor	3,968	26,353	43 (1.3)	23 (1.2)	12 (0.7)	8 (0.9)	4 (0.8)	239 (2.2)
Food Stamps								
No	21,754	171,115	83 (0.6)	87 (0.6)	94 (0.5)	97 (0.5)	99 (0.8)	276 (0.6)
Yes	3,001	17,953	17 (1.4)	13 (1.2)	6 (1.1)	3 (0.7)	1 (0.9)	236 (1.8)
Interest from Savings								
No	13,871	100,702	76 (0.7)	63 (1.0)	48 (0.8)	29 (0.8)	15 (1.8)	251 (0.9)
Yes	10,884	88,365	24 (0.5)	37 (1.0)	52 (0.9)	71 (0.9)	85 (1.9)	297 (0.7)
Document								
Poverty Level								
Not poor	14,868	113,929	59 (0.7)	80 (0.8)	88 (0.7)	92 (0.6)	94 (1.4)	284 (0.8)
Poor/near poor	3,968	26,353	41 (1.5)	20 (1.3)	12 (0.9)	8 (0.9)	6 (1.4)	234 (2.3)
Food Stamps								
No	21,754	171,115	83 (0.5)	89 (0.4)	94 (0.5)	97 (0.4)	99 (0.6)	271 (0.8)
Yes	3,001	17,953	17 (1.4)	11 (1.3)	6 (1.1)	3 (0.6)	1 (0.6)	232 (1.9)
Interest from Savings								
No	13,871	100,702	73 (0.7)	61 (0.7)	46 (0.6)	29 (0.7)	17 (0.9)	247 (0.9)
Yes	10,884	88,365	27 (0.6)	39 (0.8)	54 (0.7)	71 (0.8)	83 (1.0)	289 (0.9)
Quantitative								
Poverty Level								
Not poor	14,868	113,929	56 (0.7)	78 (1.0)	88 (0.6)	93 (0.6)	96 (1.1)	291 (0.7)
Poor/near poor	3,968	26,353	44 (1.3)	22 (1.3)	12 (1.0)	7 (1.0)	4 (1.1)	233 (2.4)
Food Stamps								
No	21,754	171,115	81 (0.6)	88 (0.6)	94 (0.5)	97 (0.4)	99 (0.6)	276 (0.7)
Yes	3,001	17,953	19 (1.2)	12 (1.2)	6 (1.1)	3 (0.6)	1 (0.7)	228 (1.9)
Interest from Savings								
No	13,871	100,702	77 (0.7)	64 (0.7)	47 (0.7)	29 (1.1)	15 (1.2)	248 (1.0)
Yes	10,884	88,365	23 (0.6)	36 (0.7)	53 (0.7)	71 (1.2)	85 (1.2)	298 (0.9)

n = sample size; WGT N = population size estimate / 1,000 (the sample sizes for subpopulations may not add up to the total sample sizes, due to missing data); CPCT = column percentage estimate; PROF = average proficiency estimate; (SE) = standard error of the estimate (the reported sample estimate can be said to be within 2 standard errors of the true population value with 95% confidence).

Source: U.S. Department of Education, National Center for Education Statistics, National Adult Literacy Survey, 1992.

TABLE 2.4

Median Weekly Wages and Average Weeks Worked in the Past 12 Months, by Literacy Levels

WAGES AND WEEKS WORKED	LITERACY LEVEL		Level 1 225 or lower		Level 2 226 to 275		Level 3 276 to 325		Level 4 326 to 375		Level 5 376 or higher	
	n	WGT N (/1,000)		(SE)		(SE)		(SE)		(SE)		(SE)
Weekly Wages	14,927	108,672										
Prose			240	(2.2)	281	(4.8)	339	(16.9)	465	(19.0)	650	(61.5)
Document			244	(5.2)	288	(8.9)	350	(0.6)	462	(28.7)	618	(34.6)
Quantitative			230	(10.5)	274	(11.4)	345	(3.8)	472	(14.9)	681	(49.5)
Weeks Worked	24,944	190,523										
Prose			19	(0.5)	27	(0.4)	35	(0.4)	38	(0.4)	44	(0.7)
Document			19	(0.5)	29	(0.3)	35	(0.4)	40	(0.4)	43	(0.8)
Quantitative			18	(0.5)	29	(0.4)	34	(0.4)	39	(0.4)	40	(0.8)

n = sample size; WGT N = population size estimate / 1,000 (the sample sizes for subpopulations may not add up to the total sample sizes, due to missing data); (SE) = standard error of the estimate (the reported sample estimate can be said tobe within 2 standard errors of the true population value with 95% confidence).

! Interpret with caution -- the nature of the sample does not allow accurate determination of the variability of this statistic.

Source: U.S. Department of Education, National Center for Education Statistics, National Adult Literacy Survey, 1992.

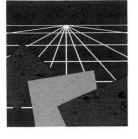

PARTICIPANTS

in the Development Process

Literacy Definition Committee

Ms. Barbara Clark
Regional Manager
Central Region
Los Angeles Public Library

Ms. Nancy Cobb
Manager
Human Resources Development Department
Nabisco Biscuit Company

Ms. Hanna Fingeret
Director
Literacy South

Ms. Evelyn Ganzglass
Director
Employment and Social Services Policy Studies
Center for Policy Research
National Governors' Association

Mr. Ronald Gillum
Director
Adult Extended Learning Services
Michigan Department of Education

Mr. Karl Haigler
President
The Salem Company

Mr. Carl Kaestle
Professor of Educational Policy Studies
Wisconsin Center for Educational Research
University of Wisconsin

Mr. Reynaldo Macías
(Liaison to the Technical Review Committee)
Professor of Education and Director
UC Linguistic Minority Research Institute
University of California, Santa Barbara

Mr. David Neice
Director of Research and Analysis Directorate
Department of the Secretary of State
Canada

Honorable Carolyn Pollan
(ex-officio member)
State Representative
Arkansas State Legislature

Ms. Lynne Robinson
Director of Support Services
Division of ACE
Sweetwater Union High School District

Mr. Anthony Sarmiento
Director
Education Department
AFL-CIO

Ms. Gail Spangenberg
Vice President and Chief Operating Officer
Business Council for Effective Literacy

Technical Review Committee

Ms. Susan Embretson
Professor
Department of Psychology
University of Kansas

Mr. Jeremy Finn
Professor
Graduate School of Education
SUNY Buffalo

Mr. Robert Glaser
Director
Learning Research and Development Center
University of Pittsburgh

Mr. Ronald Hambleton
Professor
School of Education
Laboratory of Psychometric and Evaluative Research
University of Massachusetts

Mr. Huynh Huynh
Professor
Department of Educational Psychology
University of South Carolina at Columbia

Ms. Sylvia Johnson
Professor
Howard University

Mr. Frank Schmidt
Professor
Industrial Relations and Human Resources
College of Business
University of Iowa

Mr. Richard Venezky
(Liaison to the Literacy Definition Committee)
Professor
Department of Educational Studies
University of Delaware

Literacy of Older Adults Review Group

Ms. Michele Adler
Disability Policy Analyst
Office of Assistant Secretary for Planning and Evaluation
Department of Health and Human Services

Ms. Helen Brown
(Liaison to the Literacy Definition Committee
and the Technical Review Committee)
Research Analyst/Associate
American Association of Retired Persons

Ms. Bella Jacobs
Consultant
National Council on the Aging

Mr. Robert H. Prisuta
Senior Research Associate
Research and Data Resources Department
American Association of Retired Persons

Literacy of Incarcerated Adults Review Group

Ms. Caroline Wolf Harlow
Statistician
Bureau of Justice Statistics

Mr. Christopher Koch
Education Program Specialist
Office of Correctional Education
U.S. Department of Education

Ms. Harriet Lebowitz
Social Science Research Analysis
Federal Bureau of Prisons

Mr. Ronald Pugsley
Office of Vocational and Adult Education
U.S. Department of Education

Ms. Gail Schwartz
Chief for the Office of Correctional Education
U.S. Department of Education

Test Development Consultants

Ms. Valerie de Bellis
Center for Mathematics, Science, and Computer
Education·
Rutgers University

Mr. John Dawkins
Language and Literature Department
Bucks County Community College

Ms. Harriet L. Frankel
Secondary and Higher Education Programs
Educational Testing Service

Ms. Bonnie Hole
The Bureau of Evaluation and Student Assessment
Connecticut State Department of Education

Mr. Richard Lesh
Division of Cognitive and Instructional Science
Educational Testing Service

Ms. Ave M. Merritt
Secondary and Higher Education Programs
Educational Testing Service

Mr. Peter Mosenthal
Reading and Language Arts Center
Syracuse University

Ms. Pam Smith
Secondary and Higher Education Programs
Educational Testing Service

Ms. Wallie Walker-Hammond
Secondary and Higher Education Programs
Educational Testing Service

About the Authors

Irwin S. Kirsch is project director of the National Adult Literacy
Survey and executive director of the Literacy Learning and
Assessment Group at Educational Testing Service.

Ann Jungeblut is a senior research associate at Educational
Testing Service.

Lynn Jenkins is a program administrator in the Literacy
Learning and Assessment Group at Educational Testing Service.

Andrew Kolstad is project monitor for the National Adult
Literacy Survey at the National Center for Education Statistics,
U.S. Department of Education.

U.S. GOVERNMENT PRINTING OFFICE : 1993 O - 356-371 : QL 3